THE CATHOLIC FAITH

THE CATHOLIC FAITH

AN INTRODUCTION TO THE CREEDS

STEPHEN K. RAY
R. DENNIS WALTERS

TAN Books
Gastonia, North Carolina

NIHIL OBSTAT: I have concluded that the materials presented in this work are free of doctrinal and moral errors.

Msgr. Robert Lunsford, Censor Librorum, July 17, 2006

IMPRIMATUR: Permission to publish this work is granted (cf. Can. 830, §3). Carl F. Mengeling, Bishop of Lansing, July 17, 2006

Cover Design: Caroline Green

Cover Art: Saint Peter's basilica interior, photo by Alessandro Colle/ Shutterstock

ISBN: 978-1-5051-1787-5
Kindle ISBN: 978-1-5051-1788-2
EPUB ISBN: 978-1-5051-1789-9

Published in the United States by

TAN Books

PO Box 269

Gastonia, NC 28053

www.TANBooks.com

Printed in the United States of America

CONTENTS

Chapter One

OUR "CREED-ABLE" FAITH

In *The Two Towers*, the second book of J. R. R. Tolkien's *Lord of the Rings* trilogy, the hobbits Frodo and Samwise must cross a swamp called the Dead Marshes. Their only guide is Gollum, who might kill to steal the Ring of Power that Frodo is carrying. Supposedly "tamed," Gollum promises to lead them safely across, though Sam suspects treachery. "Trust Sméagol!" Gollum urges. "He can take you through the marshes, through the mists, nice thick mists." The nearly invisible path meanders through pools and quicksand. As will-o'-the-wisps lure them toward dark water, Gollum warns: "Follow Sméagol! Don't look at lights!"

The Different Faces of Faith

The word *creed* comes into English from a Latin verb meaning "to believe." The verb is *credere*, and it has spun off many words such as *credible* (and *incredible*), *credulous*, *credit*, and so on. A creed is a statement or list of beliefs—not necessarily religious ones. But, for many moderns, there lurks a dark suspicion that creeds in general hobble the mind's instinct to range free. After all, the world is full of alluring lights.

The idea most closely linked to a creed is faith in it. Like creed, *faith* comes from another Latin verb, *fidere*, and has spun off its own set of English words including *fidelity*, *confidence*, and *fiduciary*. The underlying notion is trust. But again, as with creeds, moderns suspect that faith is dangerous because in their minds it is blind. For them, *seeing* is believing; they want hard facts backed up with plenty of evidence. The world is full of mists; people want to *know*, not trust.

But *is* faith blind? The Hebrew word for "faith" means firm or solid, like solid ground. Such ground is true because it is reliable—you can put your weight on it and you won't sink. What's more, you become firm to the extent that you put your weight on what is firm. In the snippet from *The Two Towers* that begins this chapter, Gollum knows where to find solid ground in swampy country. The Hebrew does not mean that Gollum *makes* the ground firm but only that he is trustworthy enough to locate it. Plus, when Frodo and Samwise do as he says, they stand on firm ground and are themselves firm.

Faith thus involves a personal relationship. Faith is not, says Peter Kreeft, "the relation between an intellect and an idea but the relation between an I and a Thou."[1] But a relationship includes a certain level of risk. The believer relies on the giver of a promise to deliver on it (see Gen. 15:1ff) or on the guide to know the route (Ex. 14:15–31; Deut. 1:28–32). Logically, too, a relationship means the believer accepts risk. This is what Paul means by "the obedience of faith": The believer hears the directions and acts upon them (Rom. 1:5;

---

1. Peter Kreeft, The Creed (Los Angeles: Twin Circle Publishing, 1986), 6.

16:26).[2] Once Frodo and Samwise decide to trust Gollum's promise to lead them through the Dead Marshes, they commit themselves to follow him and do what he says: "Follow Sméagol! Don't look at lights!"

Creeds and the Way Things Are

True, "faith is not science." Rather, faith doesn't use the scientific *method.* Faith does not observe, collect, measure, and analyze data. But it may use the results; scientists themselves have to believe their conclusions, as they must the principles on which science is based. But faith *is* a form of knowledge, as are judgment, wisdom, insight, intuition, and personal experience.

Faith knows by contemplating. As those who study the visual arts recognize, you know a painting the more you look at it. And the more you look at it, the more you discover about it—and often about yourself. The canvas seems to reveal, to remove the veil from itself, allowing you to discover its *mystery*—that something more that keeps pulling you back for another look.

It's the same with personalities, including your own. If you have ever studied the eyes of a loved one, you are contemplating a mystery. What you see there recedes into a deep unknown; even as you glimpse it, more awaits just beyond your look. You look again, you ponder, you ask, you listen. Mystery draws you into itself; you look away only to be

2. *Catechism of the Catholic Church* 143ff.

drawn back. Attraction gives way to knowledge, knowledge to a kind of love, and love to faith.[3]

Good as all that is, human faith cannot get far on its own. The heavens proclaim the glory of God (Ps. 19:1) and creation his existence (Rom. 1:20). But it takes a nudge from God himself to hear it. We call that nudge grace. No one can know the mind of God without it (Rom. 11:33–36), but God provides that knowledge by stimulating and guiding faith (1 Cor. 2:9–12).

People sometimes call faith a "leap," because it results in a decision to act. Faith uses what it gleans from other forms of knowledge, but it must eventually step out from the safety of observation onto the surface of mystery and trust the mystery to hold firm.

Which brings us to the creeds. The two best known and most used are the Apostles' Creed and the Nicene Creed, which most Catholics call—one, or the other, or both—simply the Creed.

Both begin with the words, "I believe in..." followed by mind-boggling statements:

- An all-powerful God created the universe.
- This God is three Persons whose Son became human through being born of a virgin.
- He was executed but rose to life again.
- There is a Holy Spirit and a Church.
- Human beings will rise after they die.
- They will live forever.

Notice the verb tenses. Certain statements happened in the

3. Ibid., 156–159.

past, others are ongoing now, and still others will happen in the future. By saying "I believe," you place your weight on these statements in the expectation that each is true.

In other words, the Creed commits you to a view of reality. This, it says, is the way things are.[4] Now, it is one thing to accept the historical statements as true and the present-tense statements as valid. But you are staking your entire destiny on what the Creed says about the future. If the past and the present statements are false, then you lose nothing if you treat the future statements as false.

A "Hierarchy" of Truths

Surprisingly, the Church has never compiled a list of everything it believes. Which beliefs are central to the Christian faith? The Catechism answers by referring to "an order or 'hierarchy' of truths."[5] Does that mean that some truths are "more true" than others? No. It means that some are closer to the core of the faith than others. The Creeds list what the most central truths are.

According to the Catechism, the core truth of Christian faith is the mystery of God as a Trinity of Persons:

> The mystery of the Most Holy Trinity is the central mystery of Christian faith and life. It is the mystery of God in himself. It is therefore the source of all the other mysteries of faith. . . . It is the most fundamental and essential teaching in the "hierarchy of the truths of

4. Ibid., 170.
5. Ibid., 90.

faith." The whole history of salvation is identical with the history of the way and the means by which the one true God, Father, Son and Holy Spirit, reveals himself to men "and reconciles and unites with himself those who turn away from sin.[6]

All other Christian beliefs "fan out" from that one.

But if the past and present statements are true, what do you make of the future ones? The Creed guides your foot onto new ground.

What the Creeds Are For

Many religions or guiding philosophies seem to do quite well without a formal creed. Judaism and Islam codify laws of behavior but allow (within limits) a fairly wide range of beliefs. Hinduism as a religion and Buddhism as an encompassing philosophy focus more on transformation through self-discipline or enlightenment than on fidelity to doctrines. Of course, there must be some beliefs or there would be no religion or universally applied philosophy:

- Buddha's Eightfold Path begins with Right Knowledge.
- Hinduism believes that the truth of life lies within the self.
- Islam proclaims "no god but Allah."

---

6. Ibid., 243.

- Judaism holds as fundamental that God is One being—himself.

Christianity is one of the few religions that has a creed with several variants. It developed for historical reasons, as explained in chapter 2. As formulated, the Creed serves four main functions.

First, it is **confessional**. By saying "I believe," you commit yourself to what the Creed says. "But faith is not an isolated act. No one can believe solely alone. You have not given yourself faith, just as you have not given yourself life."[7] You have received faith from others and should hand it on to others. The Creed unites you to a community of believers and commits you to passing it on.

Second, it is **liturgical**. *Recitation of the Creed is an act of worship.* It is part of the liturgy of baptism, where the candidate professes a personal faith, and part of the Eucharistic assembly, where the entire Church gathers to commune with God.[8]

How Many Christian Creeds Are There?

Quite a few. The New Testament alone has dozens. Here are examples of some and the forms or purposes by which creeds were expressed:

- Hymns (Phil. 2:5–11; Col. 1:15–20)
- Letters: Bishops often included statements of faith in

7. Ibid., 166.
8. Ibid., 167.

letters to local churches (e.g., Ignatius's *Letter to the Trallians* 9)

- Catechetical or instructional writings for accompanying baptism (Hippolytus's *Apostolic Tradition*)
- Apologetical creed: More formal creeds were written to combat heresies (Justin Martyr's *First Apology* 61)
- An anti-Arian creed written by Eusebius of Caesarea formed the basis of the Nicene Creed. In the West, the "Apostles' Creed" evolved from creeds written by Ambrose of Milan and Rufinus of Aquilaea
- Several local and ecumenical councils, and creeds written by popes such as Pius IV and Paul VI

Most creeds are Trinitarian in structure.
For a selected list, see Appendix 1.

Third, it is **symbolic**. The *Catechism* explains:

> The Greek word *symbolon* meant half of a broken object, for example, a seal presented as a token of recognition. The broken parts were placed together to verify the bearer's identity. The symbol of faith, then, is a sign of recognition and communion between believers. *Symbolon* also means a gathering, collection, or summary. A symbol of faith is a summary of the principal truths of the faith and therefore serves as the first and fundamental point of reference for catechesis.[9]

In the early Church, catechumens (those learning the Catholic faith with the intent of entering the Church) had

9. Ibid., 188.

to learn the Creed and recite it to the bishop before he would baptize them.

Bishop Theodore Explains Why We Recite the Creed at Baptism

Theodore was bishop of Mopsuestia (near Antioch) from 392 to 428. In this pre-baptismal instruction, he explains why the rejection of Satan is followed by a recitation of the Creed:

> But you must add "I believe," for, as St. Paul much later wrote, "whoever would draw near to God must believe that he exists." Since God is invisible by nature, to face him and promise to persevere as members of his household you need faith. The blessings that God is preparing for us in heaven by the administration of Christ our Lord, the blessings that we hope for when we present ourselves for baptism—these are invisible and indescribable, too. For this reason too we must have faith in the invisible blessings in store for us.[10]

Fourth, it is **normative**. The Creed is a "rule of faith" in two senses. One, it *defines* the faith by including what Christians believe and excluding what they do not. Two, it establishes boundaries for conduct. If you really believe that Jesus "will come to judge the living and the dead," you are likely to watch your behavior.

This book focuses on the two most common versions of

10. *Theodore of Mopsuestia, Baptismal Homily II*, 14.

the Creed, the Apostles' Creed and the Nicene Creed. After tracing the development of the Creed in chapter 2, we will discuss what the Creed says about God in chapters 3 through 5 and about mankind in chapters 6 and 7. We will reply to some common objections regarding the Creed in chapter 8. (Appendixes provide additional information, including an annotated list of creeds in appendix 1 and a glossary of terms used in this book in appendix 2.)

Chapter Two

HOW NEED BUILT THE CREED

They arrived at the Council bearing the scars of "persecutions, afflictions, imperial threats, cruelty from officials, and whatever other trial" the Arian troublemakers could inflict upon them. The Eastern bishops wrote to Pope Damasus from Constantinople explaining how the tyranny of the Arian emperor Constantius had imposed great suffering on the apostolic faith. The believers had "experienced a ferment of hatred from the heretics . . . by being stoned to death in the manner of the blessed Stephen. Others were torn to shreds by various tortures and still carry around on their bodies the marks of Christ's wounds and bruises." They had endured financial loss, fines, confiscation of property, imprisonment, and other outrages.[1] Despite these injuries—perhaps because of them—these bishops met in Constantinople in 381 to clarify and reinforce the First Council of Nicaea held fifty-six years earlier. You know the Nicene Creed we recite at Sunday Mass? Well, that statement of faith is the result of these bishops gathered in council.

---

1. "Letter of the Bishops Gathered in Constantinople" in Norman P. Tanner, ed. *Decrees of the Ecumenical Councils: Constantinople I* (Washington, D.C.: Georgetown University Press, 1990), 25ff.

The Faith of Israel: God Is One

Of all the world religions, only Judaism, Christianity, and Islam claim to be revealed by God. Revelation means that something or someone outside the visible world communicates with mankind by "pulling back the curtain" to make known things we could have never discovered with our five human senses.

The oldest of these religions is Judaism. Over a period of about 2,000 years, a nomadic tribe originating in Mesopotamia (modern day Iraq) grew into a nation with a singular destiny—to live in loving communion with the One God:

> Hear, O Israel: The Lord our God is one Lord; and you shall love the Lord your God with all your heart, and with all your soul, and with all your might (Deut. 6:4–5).

This basic statement of Israel's faith is called the *Shema Israel*, which Jews everywhere recite daily. It proclaims that the Lord is not many gods but one God, with real authority. God is Lord. This truth was addressed to all of Israel and called for a personal response of love. It was because of *his* love that this one God had chosen Israel, delivered the Israelites from slavery, and gave them a land of their own and a new way of life (Deut. 4:6–12). He chose Israel to be a nation set apart for himself (Ex. 19:4–6). He would be Israel's God (Gen. 17:7; Lev. 26:12; Jer. 11:4)—a choice he made because he loved them, not because of their merits (Deut. 7:7–10).

Other nations did not share this faith in one God. During the reign of Pharaoh Akhenaten, Egypt had experimented with faith in one god (Aten, the sun god), but that experiment was quickly crushed, largely by ancient Egyptian priests. The gods of other nations did not give or receive love, let alone mercy; they were capricious, vindictive, in conflict with other gods, and contemptuous of human beings. The *Shema* compresses in one sentence the faith, hope, and love of Israel for the one Lord. The word *creed* comes from the Latin *credo*, which means "I believe." The *Shema* was the creed of Israel.

Some Old Testament Creedal Statements

God is one: "God said to Moses, 'I AM WHO I AM.' And he said, 'Say this to the people of Israel, "I AM has sent me to you" (Ex. 3:14).

God created the universe: "In the beginning God created the heavens and the earth" (Gen. 1:1).

There is only one God: "I am the Lord, and there is no other, besides me there is no God; I gird you, though you do not know me, that men may know, from the rising of the sun and from the west, that there is none besides me" (Is. 45:5–6).

Because God is one, Israel must not worship other gods: "I am the Lord your God, who brought you out of the land of Egypt, out of the house of bondage. You shall have no gods before me" (Ex. 20:2–3).

The Faith of the Apostles: Jesus Is Lord

Jesus of Nazareth had been crucified. Based on the law of Moses, he had seemingly been discredited as the Messiah (or Anointed One): God's curse was upon anyone hanged upon a tree (Deut. 21:22–23) as Jesus had been. But rumors of his Resurrection were circulating. All of a sudden, pilgrims gathering in Jerusalem to celebrate the Sinai Covenant heard strong winds, strange languages or tongues, and an even stranger explanation of what it all meant:

> Men of Israel, hear these words: Jesus of Nazareth, a man attested to you by God with mighty works and wonders and signs which God did through him in your midst, as you yourselves know—this Jesus, delivered up according to the definite plan and foreknowledge of God, you crucified and killed by the hands of lawless men. But God raised him up, having loosed the pangs of death, because it was not possible for him to be held by it. . . . This Jesus God raised up, and of that we all are witnesses. Being therefore exalted at the right hand of God, and having received from the Father the promise of the Holy Spirit, he has poured out this which you see and hear. . . . Let all the house of Israel therefore know assuredly that God has made him both Lord and Christ, this Jesus whom you crucified (Acts 2:22–24, 32–33, 36).

Peter's words stunned his audience. He said that God, far from cursing Jesus, had it all *planned* in advance. He said that God raised Jesus from the dead, that the disciples witnessed it, that the resurrected Jesus was now sitting at the "right hand of God," a position of royal power, and that the Holy Spirit had come down in fire as at the first covenant at Mount Sinai. But there is more. By quoting Psalm 110:1—a psalm Jesus applied to himself (Matt. 24:41–45)—Peter implied that there was more to understanding God than his audience realized. For "this Jesus whom you crucified" is both Messiah (*Christos* in Greek) and Lord (*Adonai* in Hebrew).

The four Gospels (and the book of Acts) contain biographical information, but they are also proclamations of good news. They reveal who Jesus is: the long awaited Messiah (Mark 1:2–8), the fulfillment of the law and the prophets (Mark 9:2; Luke 9:28–30), the Son of God (Matt. 3:16–17; 16:16), and the sacrificial Passover Lamb (Matt. 26:28; 1 Cor. 5:7). Dead and buried, he rose from the tomb, because death could not hold him (Acts 2:24). Peter captured it nicely in a creedal statement at Caesarea Philippi: "You are the Christ, the son of the living God" (Matt. 16:16).

John's Gospel begins modestly enough: "In the beginning was the Word, and the Word was with God." Both statements are consistent with Jewish belief in the oneness of God, for the *Word*—"Wisdom" in Old Testament terms—was viewed by the Jews not as God but as an emanation of God, his power, one of his attributes. So a careful Jew could read these first two clauses serenely. But the third clause hits the horn: "and the Word was God" (literally that the Word "was being" in the beginning with God *as* God—and as to his nature, he was divine). John compounds the matter by declaring: "All things were made through him, and without him was not anything made that was made" (John 1:3). To make matters worse, John asserts that this God-Word "became flesh and dwelt among us" (John 1:14), the only Son from the Father, on whom the Holy Spirit rests (John 1:33). The Trinity is present from the outset of this Gospel.

But John is not finished yet. He recalls how Jesus identified himself as the Son who is one with the Father (10:30; 17:11), reveals the Father (6:65; 14:6), and gives the Holy Spirit (15:26). Jesus is the light of the world (9:5), the resurrection and the life (11:25), the true bread from heaven (6:33–51), the vine (15:1), the Lamb of God who takes the world's sin away (1:29, 36). Jesus existed before Abraham was born; he is the I Am (8:58; *cf.* Ex. 3:14–15)—the divine name his enemies instantly recognized. He is a king (18:33–37) from whose pierced side flowed blood and water (19:34; 1 John 5:6–8). John makes it clear: Jesus of Nazareth is God—God in the flesh.

Within twenty-five years of Jesus' Ascension, Paul vigorously affirmed the bodily Resurrection of Jesus, to which hundreds still living could attest (1 Cor. 15:5–8). Having conquered death, Jesus now sits at God's right hand as king (1 Cor. 15:25). Moreover, Jesus is the Son of God as proven by his Resurrection (Rom. 1:4), equal with the Father and the Holy Spirit (Eph. 1:2; 2 Cor. 13:14). Jesus is Christ and Lord (Phil. 2:11).

To many Jews, it seemed that Paul was twisting the *Shema* beyond recognition. In 1 Corinthians, Paul alludes to the *Shema Israel*: "For us there is one God, the Father, from whom are all things and for whom we exist" (1 Cor. 8:6). Up to this point, the Jew would have no argument with Paul. But many Jews would be aghast when Paul says in the same verse that there is "one Lord, Jesus Christ, through whom are all things and through whom we exist."

For Jews, it was one thing to claim that Jesus is the Christ (Messiah), for the Messiah was not as such divine. Nor was there any problem for Jews with saying that Jesus is a son of God; Scripture uses such expressions referring to human beings who have a special relationship with God. But to call Jesus "Lord"—*that* crossed a line. Paul is not only claiming divinity for Jesus; he is saying that the one God is somehow a plurality.

But Paul is no polytheist. For his pagan converts, the issue is their pantheon of gods; Christianity had to explain to them that there is only one God. The Father, Son, and Holy Spirit are one God, not three gods. Christians must also explain to Jews that the Trinitarian nature of God does not defy or negate the *Shema Israel*—that God is one; rather, it is a deeper understanding of the one God.

The Creed Takes Shape

The baptized have to be disciples, learners. They must be taught who Jesus is, for in baptism they "put on Christ" (Gal. 3:27). They must confess what they believe, and to do so they must have a carefully worded verbal confession to bring faith to life (Rom. 10:8–10) and enable believers to understand the truth and defend what they believe. Heresies swirled around the question of who and what Jesus Christ was. Christians needed a simple statement of their faith to counteract the insidious heresies. The apostles, who preached the message of Jesus, provided models of such confessions, often in the form of hymns that were easily memorized. Peter provided a summary of faith—elements of which still appear in creeds we recite (the italicized parts):

> *Christ also died for sins* once for all, the righteous for the unrighteous, that he might bring us to God, *being put to death in the flesh* but made alive in the spirit; in which *he went and preached to the spirits in prison*. . . . Baptism . . . now saves you, not as a removal of dirt from the body but as an appeal to God for a clear conscience, through the *resurrection of Jesus Christ, who has gone into heaven and is at the right hand of God*, with angels, authorities, and powers subject to him (1 Pet. 3:18–19, 21–22).

One of Paul's most famous "creeds" is the hymn embedded in Philippians, part of which goes:

> [Christ] emptied himself, taking the form of a servant, being *born in the likeness of men*. And being found in human form he humbled himself and became obedient unto death, even *death on a cross*. Therefore God has *highly exalted him* and bestowed on him the name which is above every name, that at the name of Jesus every knee should bow, in heaven and on earth and under the earth, and every tongue confess that *Jesus Christ is Lord*, to the glory of God the Father (Phil. 2:7–11).

Such passages suggest the shape of the earliest creeds and that they originally arose from a need and desire to compress the message of the Gospel into a simple yet profound summary, especially useful for catechumens preparing for baptism. At the Easter Vigil, catechumens were required to state their belief in what the apostles taught. During their instruction, the bishop "handed over" the creed to learn by heart. They were not to write it or reveal it to anyone, to prevent misunderstanding but were to "hand it back" (recite it) to the bishop on the day of baptism. Possibly because people memorized the creed, few written examples from the first centuries exist. But enough do exist that we can trace their development.

Since the formula of baptism was Trinitarian (Matt. 28:19), it was natural that the early creeds developed a Trinitarian structure. Typically, they used a series of short clauses, known as "articles." Two of the most ancient creeds follow this structure. The first comes from a document (roughly, A.D. 150–180) influenced by the heresy of Gnosticism. Note how it avoids calling Jesus "Son of God" or mentioning the resurrection of the body:

> [I believe] in the Father almighty and in Jesus Christ, our Savior; and in the Holy Spirit, the Paraclete in the holy Church, and in the remission of sins.

Safeguarding the "Hidden Teachings"

St. Cyril, teaching catechumens in Jerusalem in 348, explains why they must not reveal what they have learned in class to outsiders:

> Learn by heart the things that are told you, and guard

> them always. . . . After the class, if any unbeliever or catechumen tries to find out what you have learned, tell him nothing. Guard the secret. Never let anyone work it out of you, asking what harm it would do to tell him. I tell you it would do a great deal of harm; it would be like giving a sick person strong drink. Strong drink makes the patient delirious; then he dies and the doctor is blamed. In the same way, if an unbeliever or catechumen hears something divulged by a Christian, he misunderstands and scoffs at it, because there must first be faith before it is possible to understand. And if this should happen, the Christian would be condemned for betraying his trust.
>
> My brothers and sisters, you are standing at the gates of the heavenly mystery. I put you under oath to smuggle nothing out of the citadel, not because the things you are to learn are not fit to be repeated, but because your audience is not ready to understand them.[2]

A more orthodox example derives from the early third century. This early creed clearly teaches that Jesus is the Son of God and that there will be a resurrection of the body:

> I believe in God almighty; and in his only begotten Son, our Lord Jesus Christ, and in the Holy Spirit, and in the resurrection of the body [in] the holy Catholic Church.

---

2. Cyril of Jerusalem *Inaugural Catechesis*, from Anne Field, O.S.B., *From Darkness to Light: How One Became a Christian in the Early Church* (Ben Lomond, CA, Conciliar Press, 1997), p. 28.

The Gnostic-influenced creed just quoted illustrates a problem faced by the early Church: what the creed should say about Jesus. Dealing with that issue caused the creeds to balloon in the middle by adding a christological substructure.

From the time of Ignatius of Antioch (martyred around A.D. 107), Church Fathers insisted with the apostles that Jesus is fully human and fully divine. For example, Ignatius writes to the Church at Smyrna that Jesus was:

> Born and unborn, God become man, true life in death, sprung both from Mary and from God, first subject to suffering, and then incapable of it—Jesus Christ our Lord. He is really of the line of David according to the flesh, and the Son of God by the will and power of God; was really born of a Virgin.[3]

Melito of Sardis made the same point:

> Being God and likewise perfect man, he gave positive indications of his two natures: of his deity by the miracles during the three years following after his baptism, of his humanity in the thirty years that came before his baptism, during which, by reason of his condition according to the flesh, he concealed the signs of his deity, although he was the true God existing before the ages.[4]

By the time of Irenaeus of Lyons (130–200) and Tertullian (160–225), these teachings were working their way into various creeds, expanding the article on the Son into several

3. Ignatius of Antioch, *Letter to the Smyrnaeans* 1, 1.
4. Fragment in Anastasius of Sinai, *The Guide* 13.

additional articles. Tertullian in Africa promulgated one creed as follows, expanding the part about the Son:

> Believing in one God Almighty, maker of the world, and [in] his Son, Jesus Christ, born of the Virgin Mary, crucified under Pontius Pilate, on the third day brought to life from the dead, received in heaven, sitting now at the right hand of the Father [who] will come to judge the living and the dead through the resurrection of the flesh.[5]

What we now know as the Apostles' Creed began to take shape in the Church at Rome about the same time. The oldest form comes from Hippolytus of Rome around 215 in question-and-answer form, probably for the baptismal liturgy. The articles on Jesus form a short narrative sandwiched between the articles on the Father and the Holy Spirit:

> Do you believe in Christ Jesus, Son of God, Who was born by the Holy Spirit out of Mary the Virgin, and was crucified under Pontius Pilate and died and was buried, and rose on the third day alive from among the dead, and ascended into heaven, and sits at the right hand of the Father, to come to judge the living and the dead?[6]

By the end of the fourth century, this creed had assumed the shape we now have. The question-and-answer format was replaced by the introductory statement "I believe." Rufinus of Aquilaea, in his *Commentary on the Apostles' Creed*

---

5. Tertullian, *De Virginibus Velandis* 1.
6. Hippolytus, *Apostolic Tradition.*

(c. A.D. 404), includes the article "descended into hell," based on Acts 2:27 and 1 Peter 3:18–20, to make twelve articles. According to Rufinus, Ambrose of Milan, and others, each of the twelve apostles composed one article of this creed—an unlikely story, but one that Ambrose used to help catechumens memorize all twelve articles.

The Nicene Creed that Catholics recited during Mass expands the Apostles' Creed even further (the *Catechism* compares the two after paragraph 185). This Nicene Creed was hammered out in the heat of battle and over a longer period of time.

As early as Justin Martyr (martyred c. A.D. 165), the creeds were used in conflict against subversive teachings contrary to Christianity. Early controversies with Judaism brought about the Trinitarian articles that proclaim one God with distinct operations for each of the three Persons: the Father creates, the Son saves, the Holy Spirit is an advocate or helper (*paraclete* in Greek). Controversies with Gnostic and Marcionite heretics clarified that the one God created both what is seen (the physical world) and what is not seen (the spiritual realm). With Arianism, which began to spread in the early 300s, the problem was more difficult—and much more pernicious.

Arius taught that the Son of God was not eternal but a creature and therefore had a beginning. Arius was excommunicated by the Egyptian bishops in 319, but he simply went elsewhere and gathered followers, including other bishops. St. Athanasius, then a deacon in Alexandria and later a bishop there, fiercely opposed Arianism. Because of his valiant defense, Athanasius was declared a Doctor of the Church and is called "the father of orthodoxy."

In A.D. 325, Emperor Constantine called a council of bishops to settle the matter. Condemning Arius and his doctrine was the easy part. The hard part was putting together a concise and precise statement of the truth—the orthodox faith. Arius had attacked belief in the divinity of Jesus in philosophical language, asserting that the Son was not of the same nature (*ousios*) as the Father. The Nicene bishops hammered out a philosophical response: the Son is of the same nature (*homoousios*) as the Father, and therefore eternal.

Unfortunately, the matter didn't end there. Supported by the Arian emperor, Arianism nearly overwhelmed Christianity. But faithful bishops such as Epiphanius of Salamis developed creeds for their own churches to bolster orthodox teachings. Then, in 381, a Catholic emperor called a council in Constantinople to resolve the matter. For two months, 150 Eastern bishops, mentioned earlier, worked to modify the creed of Epiphanius to strengthen the articles on the three Persons, particularly the Son and the Holy Spirit. The creed we have today combines that of Nicaea with that of Epiphanius; its publication dates from the Council of Chalcedon seventy years later and is essentially the version that Catholics recite today—the Nicene Creed.

The Nicene and Constantinopolitan Creeds Compared	
CREED OF NICAEA I (325)	**CREED OF CONSTANTINOPLE (381)**
We believe in one God the Father all powerful,	We believe in one God the Father all-powerful,
maker of all things both seen and unseen.	maker of heaven and earth, and of all things both seen and unseen.
And in one Lord Jesus Christ, the Son of God, the only begotten,	And in one Lord Jesus Christ, the only begotten Son of God,
begotten from the Father, that is, from the substance of the Father,	begotten from the Father before all the ages,
God from God, light from light, true God from true God,	light from light, true God from true God,
begotten not made, consubstantial with the Father,	begotten not made, consubstantial with the Father,
through whom all things came to be, both those in heaven and those in earth;	through whom all things came to be;
for us men and for our salvation he came down and became incarnate, became human,	for us humans and for our salvation he came down from the heavens and became incarnate from the holy Spirit and the Virgin Mary, became human,
	and was crucified on our behalf under Pontius Pilate; he suffered and was buried
suffered and rose up on the third day,	and rose up on the third day in accordance with the Scriptures;
went up into the heavens,	and he went up into the heavens and is seated at the Father's right hand;

CREED OF NICAEA I (325) *(Continued)*	CREED OF CONSTANTINOPLE (381) *(Continued)*
and is coming to judge the living and the dead.	he is coming again with glory to judge the living and the dead;
And in the Holy Spirit.	his kingdom will have no end. And in the Spirit, the holy, the lordly and life-giving one, proceeding forth from the Father, co-worshiped and co-glorified with the Father and the Son, the one who spoke through the prophets;
	in one, holy, catholic, and apostolic Church.
	We confess one baptism for the forgiving of sins. We look forward to a resurrection of the dead, and life in the age to come. Amen.

Chapter Three

IN THE BEGINNING—THE FATHER

Thousands of early Christians were executed for being atheists. They were not atheists as we know them today—people who reject the existence of God. They simply rejected the false gods and idols of the pagans. And they refused especially to worship the Roman emperor as God.

Socrates, the pagan Greek philosopher, was also condemned for atheism. He firmly believed in the existence of God, but he had no interest in the conduct of the mythical gods of Greece. Rather, he was concerned about the nature, conduct, and destiny of the human person, as were most ancient "atheists."

Modern atheists are different. They reject belief in any supernatural being or authority. The Second Vatican Council divided modern atheists into two broad groups: *systematic* or theoretical atheists, and *practical* atheists. Systematic atheists believe that "freedom consists in this: that man is an end to himself and the sole maker, with supreme control of his own history."[1] This kind of atheism extends into philosophy, politics, economics, and morality. As the Council notes, it

1. Second Vatican Council, *Gaudium et Spes* 20.

may be encouraged by the technological advances of the last century or two. The Council places agnostics—those who profess that one cannot know whether God exists or not—in the systematic category.

Practical atheists act as though God doesn't exist, regardless of what they profess to believe. They may regard God as a cartoon character (a bearded old man with a halo), or simply ignore him as irrelevant. The practical atheist is unconcerned whether God exists or not, living life as though God's existence is irrelevant.

The Creed begins at this sore point for the modern mind: "We believe in God."

"We Believe In God"

If you have ever taken a humanities course in college, you have probably studied St. Thomas Aquinas's five ways for arguing for the existence of God. As logical arguments, they are practically airtight. But your teacher may have countered by saying that they don't really *prove* that God exists, because you can accept the logic of the argument and still deny God's existence.

Scripture takes a different approach. It points up at the night sky: "The heavens are telling the glory of God; and the firmament proclaims his handiwork" (Ps. 19:1). If seeing is believing, say the books of Wisdom (13:1ff) and Romans (1:18ff), examining creation indicates that there is a Creator. As part of creation, we ourselves are an argument for the existence of God. Our minds, our consciences, our thirst for the good and true and beautiful, our desire for the eternal, even our own personalities and our ability to love, communicate, create, and entertain abstract thought—they all point *up*. "Created in God's image and called to know and love him, the person who seeks God discovers certain ways of coming to know him,"[2] says the *Catechism*. Logic and observation can assure us that belief in God is not unreasonable, but they are only the start of a "conversation" with the One who reveals himself through them.

In addition to talking *to* God, we still have to talk *about* him, using the tools of logic and language. The problem is: How do we talk about God and make sense?

Theologians use analogy or comparison. Any teacher will tell you that students learn by comparing what they *do not* know with what they *do* know. If you want to explain color to a blind person, you can compare each color to a temperature: Blue is like cold, red like hot, and so on. There are obvious differences, but the similarities can explain a lot. The Bible is full of analogies about God, and the proper way of reading the Bible is to remember what the analogies really say—and what they do not.

For example, take Genesis 1:26–27, where God makes mankind in his "image and likeness." Suppose we tried to describe God's existence by comparing it with our own. We might get across what *existence* is all about; but then we would need to explain that our existence has a beginning, and God's does not. Further, God *has* to exist, whereas we do not. Or again, we could compare God's personality to our own, but the analogy breaks down quickly. Though we are able to love, think, reason, and create similarly to God, our personality

2. CCC 31.

is limited and changeable and weakened by sin. God is not limited, not changeable, and certainly not weakened by sin. Analogy lets us compare aspects of God's being with certain aspects of our own, but we cannot forget that there are both differences and similarities.

Theologians know the need to be careful when describing God. In the Middle Ages, Peter Abelard taught that when you say something affirmative about God you often have to turn around and say the opposite. Abelard called it "Yes and No." Sometimes you can affirm things about God and leave them at that; for example, that God exists—no opposite is needed. Other statements, said Abelard, call for some kind of negation. If you say that God is *everywhere* (a positive), you have to add that he is *nowhere* (a negative), since as a spirit he does not occupy space. If you say that man can know truth about God (a positive), you have to add that this knowledge can never be exhaustive (a negative).

Simply stated, the finite human mind can never know everything there is to know about an infinite God. We can know truly but not exhaustively. Aquinas pointed out that our knowledge of God takes place on two levels. One, which he called the knowledge of "apprehension," is the simple recognition of a fact. You "apprehend" something by perceiving it, acknowledging it, and making judgments about it. For example, when an old friend enters the room, you recognize his voice and appearance. Everyone can know God at this level. The other level is what Aquinas calls "comprehension," or what we would call complete understanding. No matter how well you know your friend, there is always more to know. Likewise, whatever you know and understand about

God, that knowledge and understanding will never be all-encompassing or complete.

To discuss the Creed properly, it is important to say these things at the start, just as the *Catechism* does. But the Creed itself is not making a philosophical point. Pope John Paul II said that the Creed "does not present the existence of God as a problem in its own right."[3] Rather, the Creed assumes that God exists and that God's existence is *not* a problem. God has revealed himself in creation, in his word, and in the teaching of his Church. The Creed does not present an argument but makes a profession. By it:

> We respond to God who has revealed himself. By professing we become sharers in the truth that God has revealed, and we express it as the content of our conviction. He who reveals himself not only makes it possible for us to know that he exists, but he also enables us to know who he is, and also how he is.[4]

How Can We Speak about God?

God transcends all creatures. We must therefore continually purify our language of everything in it that is limited, image-bound, or imperfect if we are not to confuse our image of God—"the inexpressible, the incomprehensible, the invisible, the ungraspable"—with our human representations. Our words always fall short of the mystery of God.

Admittedly, in speaking about God like this, our

3. John Paul II, general audience of July 31, 1985.
4. Ibid.

language is using modes of expression; nevertheless, it really does attain to God himself, though unable to express him in his infinite simplicity. Likewise, we must recall that "between Creator and creature no similitude can be expressed without implying an even greater dissimilitude" and that "concerning God, we cannot grasp what he is but only what he is not, and how other beings stand in relation to him."[5]

"We Believe in One God"

When we consult any good Bible dictionary, we discover that in the Old Testament God has many names.

- *El* is a generic name for deity used by many Near Eastern cultures.
- Another name was *Elohim*, a plural form of *El* but usually singular in meaning.
- A third name, *Elyon* or the "Most High," is mainly a poetic title.
- A fourth name, *Shaddai* (the "all-powerful") appears as a divine name in the era before Moses.

Behind such names one might detect a suspicion of multiple gods, but other phrases clarify which God is paramount: "God has taken his place in the divine council; in the midst of the gods he holds judgment" (Ps. 82:1); "the Lord is a great God and a great King above all gods" (Ps. 95:3). Israelites believed in one God (Deut. 6:4), but they sometimes hedged their bets by worshiping pagan gods. Stories as early

5. CCC 42–43.

as Rachel stealing her father's household gods (Gen. 31:19–34) or as late as the Maccabean soldiers carrying charms of foreign gods into battle (2 Mac. 12:38–45), point to the trouble Israel had freeing itself from the worship of other gods besides the one true God.

But one particular name for God stands out as *the* name: YHWH, typically spelled *Yahweh* and usually translated "I AM WHO I AM." At the time of Jesus the name YHWH was considered so sacred that people could not say it or write it, so they used substitutes such as *Adonai* (Lord). God revealed his name YHWH to Moses at the burning bush, and the name needed no clarification. The Elohim (gods) might or might not exist, but there was only one Yahweh. Whatever else they believed about the existence of other gods, none could hold a candle to the *One*. The belief of Israel was fixed: Yahweh alone is Lord (Is. 42:8; 45:12–21); all the other gods are nothing more than hollow idols (Ps. 115:4–6; 135:15–18).

We often see references to the three monotheistic religions—Judaism, Christianity, and Islam—as if all three religions believe in the oneness of God in pretty much the same way. That idea is misleading.

For Judaism and Islam, God's singleness is at the core of God, unlike Christianity's belief in a triune God, whose being contains plurality. For both Judaism and Islam, the Christian ascription of divinity to the Son and the Spirit is a kind of polytheism. In response to the Christian claim that Jesus is Lord, Jewish texts condemned as *minim* (heretics) those who claim more than one power in heaven. And the Qur'an denies divine status to Jesus precisely because it does not suit Allah, nor is it appropriate for him to have associates.

For both Judaism and Islam, "one God" means that God is alone. Not only is there no one like him, but he is by himself, solitary, eternally apart, completely other.

For Christians there is one God, but the one God is made up of three distinct Persons. Through Jesus Christ, the oneness of God is revealed differently than in Judaism and Islam. Christians are baptized in the name (singular) of the Father and of the Son and of the Holy Spirit (Matt. 28:19). The Father reveals the Son (Matt. 3:17; 17:5), and the Son reveals the Father (Matt. 11:27; John 1:18); both reveal the Holy Spirit, who in turn reveals them (John 15:26; 16:13–14). The Father and the Son are one (John 10:30). Both the Son and the Spirit proceed from the Father (John 8:42; 15:26). God's oneness has a three-ness about it.

Early Church councils coined the word *Trinity* to express the idea of "three-in-one." Christians do not believe in three gods but one God in three Persons. The Persons don't share divinity by splitting it up among themselves; "each of them is God whole and entire."[6] Straining for clear and exact language, early councils taught that "the Father is what the Son is, the Son is what the Father is, and the Father and the Son are what the Holy Spirit is"[7]—that is, by nature one God. Some argue that the Father, the Son, and the Spirit are simply different modes or manifestations of one person, as if God wears three different masks as occasion demands. (The early Church branded this viewpoint as heresy more than a

6. Ibid., 253.

7. Council of Toledo XI, 675.

century before the Trinity was officially defined.) "God is one but not solitary," said the creed of Pope Damasus.

> "Father," "Son," "Holy Spirit" are not simply names designating modalities of the divine being, for they are really distinct from one another . . . in their relations of origin: "It is the Father who generates, the Son who is begotten, and the Holy Spirit who proceeds." The divine Unity is Triune.[8]

The names of the three Persons express the most intimate of relationships—three distinct Persons who are wholly "in" one another (see John 14:10). Again, one God in three Persons; three Persons as one God.

The way we experience the work of the Holy Trinity—how God "manages" his affairs, so to speak—is called the divine *economy*. Here, too, we see that God is one and yet three. In this economy, the three Persons act in common but each according to his own "unique personal property." Who creates the universe? The Trinity does. But the Church asserts, following the New Testament, "one God and Father *from* whom all things are, and one Lord Jesus Christ, *through* whom all things are, and one Holy Spirit *in* whom all things are."[9]

"We Believe in the Father"

"Any stud can sire a child," the saying goes. "It takes a real man to father one." Our culture has no trouble with

---

8. CCC 254; *cf.* Lateran Council IV, 1215.
9. Council of Constantinople II.

reproductive biology, but it has a terrible time with fatherhood, because so many men have failed as fathers. The Father is the first Person of the Trinity, but modern problems with the perception of fatherhood might lead to a false idea of God's Fatherhood. God is the model of fatherhood, but if we use our personal experience of fatherhood alone as a model for God's Fatherhood, it could lead to faulty conclusions. According to Paul, it is God who is the Father "from whom every family in heaven and on earth is named" (Eph. 3:15). God is the ultimate model of fatherhood. Pope John Paul II said that God's paternity starts first of all within the Trinity.[10] To understand God as Father, we need to view it from inside the Holy Trinity.

When Jesus, the Son, describes his Father in the Gospels, he uses a language of relationship, not biology. The Father is not older than the Son, since the Son was with the Father "in the beginning" (John 1:2). The Father "generates" the Son, who "eternally proceeds" or "comes out" of the Father and returns to him (John 1:14; 16:28). Because the Father and the Son are one (John 10:30), whoever sees the Son sees the Father, because they are "in" one another (John 10:38; 14:8–11, 20; 16:3; 17:21).

Likewise, Jesus speaks of the Son's relationship to the Father as subordinate. The Father is "greater" than the Son (John 14:28), who acts only in accord with the Father's authority (John 5:19, 36; 12:49–50). For example, because the Father is always working, the Son works even on the Sabbath (John 5:17). The Father sends the Son on the mission of salvation (John 8:42; 18:11; 20:21), and his will governs

10. John Paul II, general audience of October 16, 1985.

its execution (Matt. 26:39, 42; Mark 14:36; Luke 22:42). Yet the Father gives judgment—and indeed all things—to the Son (Matt. 25:31–46; John 5:22; 13:3; 16:15). The relationship of the Father with the Son is intimate and eternal. The Father is always with the Son (John 16:32), always knows him (John 17:25), always loves him (John 3:35; 5:20; 10:15, 17; 15:9; 17:24), always receives and gives honor and glory to him (John 8:53–54; 12:26; 14:13; 17:1, 5), always bears witness to him (Matt. 3:16–17; John 5:37; 6:27; 8:18), and continually hears his prayer (John 11:41; 14:16). The Father has and gives life (John 5:21, 26; 6:40). He also sends the Spirit (John 14:16), who proceeds from him (John 15:26).

Jesus distinguishes his unique relationship with the Father from that of his disciples (John 20:17), though he encourages them to approach God as their Father. Those who do the will of the Father can claim to be in his family (Matt. 12:50) and in prayer should address him as Father (Matt. 6:9–13; Luke 11:2). The Father lives in heaven but cares for us on Earth (Matt. 6:31–33). The temple was the Father's "house" (Luke 2:49) and had to be treated respectfully (John 2:16)—a figure that Paul applies to the person, especially the body, of the disciple (1 Cor. 6:19) and the Church (Eph. 2:19–22).

The Father reveals himself to mankind through the Son (John 14:6–7, 24; 16:25; Matt. 11:27; 16:17; Heb. 1:1–2). The Father's will governs all that happens (Matt. 10:29). He loves those who love the Son (John 14:23; 16:27). He gives good gifts (including the Holy Spirit), provides for daily needs (Matt. 6:8–34; Luke 11:13), provides the bread from heaven (John 6:32), and answers those who agree in prayer in the Son's name (Matt. 18:19; John 16:23).

The Son's disciples must imitate the perfection of the Father (Matt. 5:48; Luke 6:36), who rewards those who do his will (Matt. 6:1–6, 18; 7:21; 12:50; 13:43) and punishes those who do not (Matt. 13:49–50). The Father forgives those who forgive others (Matt. 6:9, 14–15) and withholds forgiveness from those who refuse to forgive (Matt. 18:21–35; Mark 11:25); indeed, the Father is eager to forgive and restore (Luke 15:3–32). The Father is glorified or hated by those who glorify or hate the Son (John 15:8; 15:23–24); in turn, the Son acknowledges or denies before the Father those who acknowledge or deny him (Matt. 10:32–33; Mark 8:38; Luke 9:26). The Father has prepared an eternal destiny for the disciples of the Son (Matt. 20:23; John 14:1ff), the kingdom of God (Luke 12:32; 22:28–30), and only he knows when it will come (Matt. 24:36; Mark 13:32).

Some people object to God portrayed in male terms. Such a portrait, they say, arose within a male-dominated society and ignores God's "feminine characteristics." God does indeed have maternal qualities, such as the kind of maternal tenderness Jesus expressed when lamenting over Jerusalem (Matt. 23:37). Some theologians would like to replace the word *Father* in the Creed with titles such as Creator, Mother, or even Father-Mother. But gender-specific language about God is analogical.

Is God Male?

By calling God "Father," the language of faith indicates two main things: that God is the first origin of everything and transcendent authority and that he is at the same time goodness and loving care for all his children. God's parental tenderness can also be expressed by the image of motherhood, which emphasizes God's immanence, the intimacy between Creator and creature.

The language of faith thus draws on the human experience of parents, who are in a way the first representatives of God for man. But this experience also tells us that human parents are fallible and can disfigure the face of fatherhood and motherhood. We ought therefore to recall that God transcends the human distinction between the sexes. He is neither man nor woman: He is God. He also transcends human fatherhood and motherhood, although he is their origin and standard: No one is father as God is Father.[11]

When we discuss the qualities of God, we must remember he is pure spirit, neither male nor female. And we must make no mistake about it; the revelation of God in Scripture refers to God as *he*—using male and fatherly terms. Within the limitations of language we have to be faithful to Scripture when talking about God and find a way of talking about him that properly conveys his Person. For its part, the Creed simply points to the language that Jesus himself used.

"We Believe in One God . . .The All-Powerful Maker"

Enter an Eastern-rite Catholic or an Orthodox church and you'll probably see a huge icon of the *Pantokrator* looking down at you from the dome. The image is usually of a young

11. CCC 239.

man whose physique, gaze, and gesture convey power, majesty, authority, and divine presence. *Pantokrator* is the Greek word for "all-powerful" or "almighty" used in Scripture and the first line of the Nicene Creed. As we saw in the previous chapter, the earliest creeds referred to God as "the almighty" or "all-powerful." The concept is as old as Scripture. In the beginning, God simply spoke and the universe was created (Gen. 1). During the Exodus, God proved to be more powerful than all of the Egyptian gods and led Israel through the Red Sea to freedom (Ex. 3–14). To the Psalmist and the prophets, God is "Lord of Hosts," a Hebraism for "all-powerful" (e.g., Psalm 24:10; Is. 6:3; Jer. 31:35; Zech. 1:7–16). The angel Gabriel assures Mary that "with God nothing will be impossible" (Luke 1:37). For Paul, God's power is visible in creation (Rom. 1:20), history (Rom. 9:16–26), and Christ's resurrection from the dead (Rom. 8:11; Gal. 1:1). The book of Revelation specifically calls God "the almighty" at least nine times.

God's Oneness means that all power in the universe resides in him alone. That the One is also Father means that God is both intelligent and can choose to do some things and not to do others, depending on the welfare of the creatures he "fathers."

For example, God has the option of preventing or allowing circumstances that, from the creature's viewpoint, are evil, like massacres. Does this mean that God, with unbridled power, conspires with evil? Or does this suggest that a Father with unlimited capacity to love nevertheless is somehow unable to prevent it? Christians cannot accept either alternative. Jesus himself refers to God's power when he prays to the

Father to spare him from death. Yet his prayer ends with submission to the Father's will (Mark 14:36). We don't begin to fully understand God's viewpoint or his ways (Rom. 11:33). But believers are assured that in the long run everything will work out well for those who love and cooperate with God and live according to his purpose (Rom. 8:28–39).

God can bring good out of evil (Gen. 50:20).

In the Creed, God's power is shown through his ability to create. Genesis begins with the Spirit "hovering" over the sea (the chaos). But unlike the Babylonian god Marduk, who creates by slaying the dragon of chaos Tiamat, God breathes a word and the cosmos takes shape. God alone creates. Though the Genesis account is consistent with the idea of creation from nothing (a Greek philosophical concept that appears late in the Old Testament), the vision of a formless and empty void is the way the Hebrew imagination explained the idea of nothingness.

This making is not something God does once and then retires to let nature take its course. In Genesis, God's Spirit hovers over the waters as a "beginning," a first cause. His Spirit is a continuing cause, since God creates all the time. He makes "heaven and earth" (the physical creation), gives breath to all things (Ps. 104:30), raises the dead to life (Rom. 8:11), and prepares a new heaven and a new earth (Rev. 21:1ff). The New Testament informs us that each Person of the Trinity actively participates in creation. The Father works even on the Sabbath, and the Son works likewise (John 5:16–18). The Father creates through his Son (Heb. 1:2ff), the Word (John 1:3ff), in whom we become new creations in Christ

Did God "Retire" after Creating the World?

Some people think that God is no longer active in the world he created. The analogy of the "divine watchmaker" who "winds up" the universe and then lets it wind down by itself was invented to maintain that God is no longer present and involved. The idea has taken on a variety of forms in modern times. To this, Psalm 104 replies:

> O Lord, how manifold are thy works! In wisdom hast thou made them all; the earth is full of thy creatures. . . . These all look to thee, to give them their food in due season. When thou givest to them, they gather it up; when thou openest thy hand, they are filled with good things. When thou hidest thy face, they are dismayed; when thou takest away their breath, they die and return to their dust. When thou sendest forth thy Spirit, they are created; and thou renewest the face of the ground. May the glory of the Lord endure for ever, may the Lord rejoice in his works, who looks on the earth and it trembles, who touches the mountains and they smoke! (Psalm 104:24, 27–32).

Scripture constantly informs us that God is continually engaged with and active in his creation.

(2 Cor. 5:17; Gal. 6:15). The Father creates through and for the Son (Col. 1:15–16), the beginning and end of all things (Rev. 2:16; 22:13).

In addition to creating "heaven and earth," the Father creates "all things visible and invisible." The Creed is not merely repeating itself here, but it is defining the scope of creation.

This definition is important for modern Christians. Ancient people had no problem believing in spiritual realities—heaven, hell, angels, demons, and the immortality of the human soul. One doesn't have to be Christian to believe in spirits. Most ancients not only believed in the reality of spirits, but they thought (as Plato did) that such things were more "real" and more important than physical realities. But they had trouble believing that the physical creation was good and created by the same God who created the spiritual realm.

By contrast, modern people tend to have difficulty believing that spiritual beings exist at all. Our modern scientific society tends to scoff at the idea of angels and demons. Even the human soul is reduced to little more than neurological reactions to stimuli. Technology and the advancements of science have wrongly convinced many that "what you see is what you get"—that the material realm of the five senses is all that exists. By saying that God created both the visible *and* invisible worlds, the Creed refutes the popular views of both the ancient and modern worlds. It blasts a clarion call proclaiming that God's universe is far more than what particle physicists or deep-space astronomers can perceive or imagine.

The Creed, then, opens a new world to modern man, in stark contrast to the world portrayed by our secular and material society.

Following the Scriptures, the Creed gives the only reliable explanation of existence, both of the seen and unseen worlds.

What the Creed says about the Father also applies to the other two Persons of the Trinity, each according to "his own unique personal property." In the next chapters we consider distinctions and activities proper to the Son and to the Spirit.

Chapter Four

"WHO DO *YOU* SAY I AM?"—THE SON

About A.D. 320 , a priest named Arius from Alexandria, Egypt, was writing to his bishop hoping to win approval for some strange new ideas:

> We know one God—alone unbegotten, alone everlasting, alone without beginning . . . begot an only begotten Son before eternal times . . . an immutable and unchangeable *perfect creature* of God. . . . But the Son, begotten by the Father, created and founded before the ages, [did not exist] before he was begotten. . . . For he is *not everlasting or co-everlasting or unbegotten with the Father. Nor does he have being [equal] with the Father.*[1]

Arius opposed the Church, teaching instead that Jesus was a creature. Hugely popular, Arius was eloquent and claimed to have logic, Scripture, and the support of the people behind him. But his teaching was heresy, and he was excommunicated.

1. From a letter by Arius to Alexander of Alexandria, in William C. Rusch, *The Trinitarian Controversy* (Minneapolis, Minn.: Augsburg Fortress, 1990), 31 (emphasis added).

Even so, his heresy swept through the Church like a raging fire.

To Arius, the Father *alone* was God. Arius thought the Church was confused: How could the Father and Son both be God if there is only one God? So he invented a divine creature, a kind of half-God, which he called the *Logos* or Word. Arianism ravaged whole nations, upsetting the empire and nearly destroying the ancient Church. The emperor tried to force it down the bishops' throats, leading to St. Jerome's lament, "The whole world groaned and was astonished to find itself Arian."[2] Only a few bishops (St. Athanasius, for example) fought back. The battle raged for more than a century.

The middle portion of the Nicene Creed was written primarily as a response to the Arian heresy. The Creed insists upon two crucial facts: that Jesus is fully God and that Jesus is fully human.

Jesus Is Fully God

To get the point across that Jesus is completely God, the Creed draws descriptions from Scripture, piling phrase upon phrase, each one turning this jewel of a mystery to reveal another facet. Earlier, this book referred to analogy—essentially a resemblance in particulars between things otherwise unlike. That approach is needed to sort out the literal language from the analogical in what follows.

---

2. Jerome, *Dialogus contra Luciferianos* 19.

"We Believe in One Lord, Jesus Christ"

The article about Jesus begins very much like the Creed's opening words. Just as we believe in one God, the Father, so we believe in one Lord, Jesus Christ.

Modern Catholics tend to swallow the statement in one gulp, but to the framers of the Creed each word was a meal in itself. Consider this:

- The key to the statement is the word *one*. Here, the Creed explains the term "Lord Jesus Christ"—there is only one of him. But as the Creed makes clear, the "one" Father shares the same nature as the "one" Son and the "one" Spirit. Compare it with the word *only* in other parts of the Creed to see how strongly it emphasizes the unity of God.
- The title *Lord* in Greek can mean a variety of things depending on its context. The Greek word is *kyrios*, and in ordinary speech it could be translated "sir." It can also refer to the head of a family (see 1 Pet. 3:6), a landowner or slave owner, a king, or even one of the gods. Paul seems to have that in mind when he remarked that, though there are many so-called gods and lords, there is only one God, the Father, and one Lord, Jesus Christ (1 Cor. 8:5–6). The Creed's phrasing is nearly identical to Paul's.
- The name *Jesus* is far more than simply the name of a first-century man. It is the Greek form of the Hebrew *Yeshua* and was the name of the Old Testament hero Joshua. The name itself means "Yahweh is salvation" or "Yahweh saves." Thus, Joseph

learned in a dream that Mary's child would be called Jesus, because he would save his people from their sins (Matt. 1:21).

- The term *Christ* in Greek is *Christos*, a translation of the Hebrew word for "Messiah" or "Anointed." It is not Jesus' last name but his title. The term was originally applied to the king (Saul and David were anointed by Samuel). That explains why Gabriel spoke to Mary of Jesus' kingly power. Everyone hoped the Messiah would bring peace, liberation, and the return of the true priesthood. The New Testament shows Jesus being very careful about revealing his identity (Mark 8:29–30), yet he praised Peter for recognizing him as the Messiah (Matt. 16:15–17). And he acknowledged it before his Jewish and Roman captors (Mark 14:61–62; Matt. 27:17, 22). At Pentecost, Peter announced that Jesus was both Lord and Christ (Acts 2:36).

"The Only Begotten Son of God, Born of the Father Before All Ages"

With these words, we run into a mix of literal and figurative language.

In the Old Testament, the expression "son of God" had several meanings. It could refer to superhuman beings or angels (Gen. 6:2, 4; Job 1:6), a devout person (Wis. 2:13–18), or a king (Ps. 2:7; 2 Sam. 7:14). Usually, it meant the people of Israel as a whole, whom God called his first-born son (Ex. 4:22; Wis. 18:13; Jer. 31:9), "adopted" through the covenant into God's "family" (Deut. 14:1–2; Is. 43:6; Hos. 11:1–4). While Jews might regard themselves as God's children and address God as Father, the title was formal and not intimate (Sir. 23:1).

Jesus, on the other hand, is uniquely intimate with the Father. Jesus called God *Abba* or "Daddy" (Mark 14:36), and claimed a unique relationship to the Father in heaven (e.g., Matt. 10:32–33; 20:23; Luke 22:29). Jesus said he is the Father's "only Son" sent to save the world (John 3:16–18). He and the Father are one (John 10:30) and work jointly, even on the Sabbath (John 5:17); whoever has seen the Son has seen the Father (John 8:19; 14:9).

Of himself Jesus said, "All things have been delivered to me by my Father; and no one knows the Son except the Father, and no one knows the Father except the Son and any one to whom the Son chooses to reveal him" (Matt. 11:27). Jesus is the "beloved Son" revealed by the Father at his baptism (Matt. 3:17; Mark 1:11; Luke 3:22) and Transfiguration (Matt. 17:5; Mark 9:8; Luke 9:35). John says repeatedly that Jesus is the "only Son" of God (John 1:14, 18; 3:16, 18; 1 John 4:9).

The rest of the New Testament agrees. Jesus is the "beloved Son" (2 Pet. 1:17) to whom God bears witness (1 John 5:9–10). The Son has the role of a prophet through whom the revelation of God is spoken to the churches (Rev. 2:18) and the world at large (Heb. 1:2). The Son is both the sacrifice sent to die for the world (Rom. 5:10; 8:32) and the high priest who offers it (Heb. 4:14; 5:5; 7:3). The Father gives this priestly role to the Son (Heb. 7:28). The Son is also king (Heb. 1:8) and inherits everything and places everything (including death) under the Father's feet (1 Cor. 15:24–28).

As to the nature of the Son, he is higher than the angels, the image of the Father, eternal, and the person through whom the Father created the world (Heb. 1:1–3). His Resurrection proves that he comes from heaven (1 Thess. 1:10). As the Father's Son, Jesus is savior of the world, capable of giving not only eternal life (1 John 4:9, 14) but the Father himself (1 John 1:3; 2:23). Indeed, Jesus is Son of God and God the Son—true God, eternal life itself (1 John 5:20).

For the early Church, it was one thing for the New Testament to refer to Jesus as the Son; it was quite another thing to define clearly what "the Son" means. The Church needed a vocabulary to even talk about it. Scripture says that God is one. But how is that possible if Yahweh has a Son? Some answered that "Son of God" must mean that the one God has three different ways or modes of showing himself: Sometimes he manifested himself as Father, sometimes as Son, and sometimes as Holy Spirit.

That made nonsense of the Scripture passages where the three Persons are clearly distinguished, yet the heresy (called Modalism because God was presumed to have different "modes" of acting) took hold and is taught by some Pentecostal groups today.

Others, mainly Arians, said the Son is a creature and denied his divinity, appealing to Greek philosophy to explain why. But this ignored Scripture passages that portrayed the Son as eternal and one with the Father by nature. The battle with Arius did have one advantage, though—his philosophical terminology forced the Church to clarify its language about the Son, even suggesting a theatrical term such as *persona*. Using philosophy as a tool, the Church could talk about persons and natures and being, explaining more precisely the biblical view of the one God.

As for the figurative language of the Bible, Scripture talks about God "begetting" the Son (Heb. 1:5, quoting Ps. 2:7); the Son is the "only begotten from" the Father (John 1:14). Earthly fathers beget sons through sexual generation. Fathers are older than their sons, but they do share human nature. They are also different entities—the father is one man, the son another. Applied to God, that analogy would seem to argue for three gods, something no Christian could accept.

In John's Gospel we see what "begetting" means. Harking back to the Genesis story of creation, John places the Word (Jesus) "in the beginning," that is, before the creation of the universe: "The Word was with God."

John twice identifies that Word as the *only begotten* Son who "was coming" into time, taking on human flesh—human nature. The Son's "begetting" is eternal—or, according to a literal translation of the Greek, "out of the Father before all eons." From all eternity and without a starting point the Son is generated, begotten from the Father. A human son has a starting point from which he begins to exist. Not so for the Son of God. The New Testament emphasizes the existence of the Son in the beginning (John 1:1). The Son is "before all things" and in him "all things hold together"; he "is the beginning" in whom "the fullness of God was pleased to dwell" (Col. 1:17–19).

In short, the begetting does not happen physically at

the moment of incarnation but is a spiritual fact, an eternal and ongoing reality with no starting point. It happens *within* God, not *between* God and something outside of him. The language of human sexual generation is metaphorical, intended to convey an eternal mystery that cannot be described literally.

"God from God, Light from Light, True God from True God, Begotten, Not Made, Consubstantial With the Father; Through Him All Things Were Made"

The New Testament insists that Jesus of Nazareth is God. John begins his Gospel with "the word was God" and ends with Doubting Thomas's words "My Lord and my God!" (John 20:28). A mere twenty years after the Resurrection, Paul can write to "the church of the Thessalonians in God the Father and the Lord Jesus Christ" (1 Thess. 1:1), where Paul places Jesus on the same level as the Father. "For us," he writes the Corinthians, "there is one God, the Father, from whom are all things and for whom we exist, and one Lord, Jesus Christ, through whom are all things and through whom we exist" (1 Cor. 8:6). Jesus is "in the form of God" (Phil. 2:6); he is the image of God in the flesh, and all the fullness of God dwells in him (Col. 1:19; 2:9). The writer of Revelation three times applies a title to Jesus that Isaiah used of Yahweh: "I am the first and I am the last; besides me there is no god" (Is. 44:6; *cf.* Rev. 1:8; 2:16; 22:13).

Long before the Nicene Creed was written, the early Church Fathers likewise insisted that Jesus of Nazareth is God. In the early second century, Ignatius of Antioch refers to "Jesus Christ our God."[3] In 189, Irenaeus of Lyons writes of "Jesus Christ our Lord and God," adding that "what cannot be said of anyone else who ever lived, that he is himself in his own right God and Lord . . . may be seen by all who have attained to even a small portion of the truth."[4] Tertullian, in A.D. 210, writes that Jesus is both "man and God."[5] "Although he was God, he took flesh," wrote Origen, "and having been made man, he remained what he was: God."[6]

So a long tradition of teaching lay behind the Creed's proclamation that the Son is God. But the Arians looked for wiggle room. They could agree that the Son is "God from God, light from light"—that, after all, is scriptural language. But, in attempting to defend God's unity, Arians said that the Son must be a lower-level or second-tier God below the Father. That is why the Creed next says "true (or real) God from true God." Arians could not agree with that, because it puts the Son on the same level as the Father. But there was more. To emphasize that the Son is not a creature, the Creed adds "begotten, not made."

So far, the Creed sticks to biblical language. But at this point, the Creed departs from biblical terminology to deal with Arianism on its own terms—using the word *consubstantial*, or "one in being"—because Arius taught that the Son is a creature, not like or of the same "substance" as the Father, and that there had to be a time when he did not exist.

The Creed suddenly injects the philosophical term

3. Ignatius of Antioch, *Letter to the Ephesians* 1.
4. Irenaeus of Lyons, *Against Heresies* 1:10:1.
5. Tertullian, *The Flesh of Christ* 5:6–7.
6. Origen, *The Fundamental Doctrines* 1:0:4.

consubstantial into otherwise biblical phrasing because the bishops at the Council of Nicaea considered themselves to be correcting a distortion, not inventing a new doctrine. They had to use the philosophical language of being because that had become the language of analysis, and Scripture did not provide any term precise enough to say what they thought needed saying. They used the term *homoousios* ("same in being") to assert the unity of the Father and the Son. In spite of the philosophical wording, the term means essentially the same as the biblical terms that came before it—the Son is God, equal in nature to the Father.

As a final stroke against Arius, the Creed adds an expression that removes the Son from things made. In Greek thought, creation is the work of a *Demiurge*, a kind of half-god created to give shape to formless matter. Arius and his followers thought Scripture supported that Greek understanding. He quoted Proverbs 8:22–31 and Sirach 24:3–9, which suggest that Yahweh created Wisdom (the Son) before all time, and Wisdom then shaped the universe. He also appealed to Paul, since Colossians 1:15 refers to the Son as the "first-born of all creation." In response, the Church Fathers held that the Son has nothing in common with a Greek-styled *Demiurge*. Colossians, for example, goes on to say that "in him *all things were created*, in heaven and on earth, visible and invisible, whether thrones or dominions or principalities or authorities—all things were created through him and for him" (Col. 1:16).

If "all things" are created through and for the Son, then the Son, who pre-existed all things (Col. 1:17), cannot be one of the things created. Other New Testament passages confirm this. "All things were made through him, and without him was not anything made that was made" (John 1:3). The Son, through whom creation is made, bears "the very stamp" of God's nature (Heb. 1:3) and is eternal (Heb. 1:8–12). The phrase "first-born of all creation" did not refer to him as a *creature*; rather, using the Jewish terminology of the first-born, it referred to a position—the Son's position as supreme master of all his creation.

An Iota of Difference

Ever hear someone say that something doesn't make "an iota of difference"? Here is how that expression came about.

The Greek text of the Nicene Creed contained a particular technical term to refer to the nature of the Son in relation to that of the Father: *homo-ousios*, meaning "the same in being." The Creed used that term to correct the teachings of the heretic Arius, who held that the Son was a kind of lesser god, a creature divine but not eternal, not the same in being with the Father.

The two positions contradicted each other, and neither side could convince the other.

To resolve things, some Eastern bishops, influenced by Arianism, tried a compromise. In Greek, the letter *i* (*iota*) inserted in the right place can change the meaning of a word. So the adjective *homos* (meaning "the same" or "identical") became *homoios* ("similar")—thus, *homo-ousios* ("the *same* in being") became *homoi-ousios* ("*similar* in being"). That tiny iota meant that the persons of the Father and the Son were distinct but were similar in their divinity.

That iota didn't make enough of a difference. The wording was still too vague, so the compromise was dropped. The Creed as published at Constantinople in 381 kept to the older Nicene term, *homo-ousios*. The Father and the Son share the same nature, not two similar ones.

Jesus Is Completely Human

As the ancient mind had a hard time believing that Jesus of Nazareth is God in the flesh, it had an equally hard time swallowing the idea that the Son of God is at the same time completely human.[7] If one starts with the assumption that the physical universe is evil, as Greeks often did, then one might deny Jesus' humanity altogether (as the heretical Gnostics did) or teach that his humanity was an illusion (as the Docetists did).

If one *were* willing to accept Jesus' humanity, one might think he had no real emotions (Stoics), or that he had no human soul (Alexandrians), or that his humanity was subsumed into his divinity (certain Greek monks), or even that there were two of him in one body (Nestorians). For most ancient people, it would have been easier to believe that he was one or the other—God or man—but not *both* at the same time.

In highlighting Jesus' life, the Creed turns from the divinity to the humanity of the Son of God. Deep waters flow beneath the creedal narrative.

---

7. CCC 464–469.

"For Us Men and for Our Salvation He Came down from Heaven"

The Psalms are filled with pleas for God to come down and save mankind. "O that deliverance for Israel would come out of Zion!" (Ps. 14:7). "Bow thy heavens, O Lord, and come down!" (Ps. 144:5). "Stir up thy might, and come to save us!" (Ps. 80:2). The Psalmist knows that he needs salvation because of sin, which is too heavy for him to bear (Ps. 51:1–3); he is a worm (Ps. 22:6) and despised (Ps. 119:141), yet God notices him (Ps. 138; 139). In the New Testament the following words are applied to Christ and actually put in his mouth. "Then I said, 'Lo, I have come to do thy will, O God,' as it is written of me in the roll of the book" (Heb. 10:7; *cf.* Ps. 40:7–8). God descends from heaven with lightning and thunder (Ps. 18:6–13; 102:18–19).

The Psalmist also asks a question very much on our own mind: "What is man that thou art mindful of him, and the son of man that thou dost care for him?" (Ps. 8:4). How do *we* rate? We're one species of animal on a very small planet, and it seems that our very existence and our sin infect the rest of the universe—a sentiment echoed in the Bible (Gen. 3:17–18). All of creation groans in futility waiting for God to release it from its bondage to decay (Rom. 8:19–23).

Modern man asks why God, if he actually exists, would care about our fate. Why should God care about a speck of dust in the universe?

Yet if Scripture has any story to tell, it is about how God loves us and *for us men and for our salvation* God intervenes time and time again to save us. The word *salvation* means many things in the Old Testament: friendship with God, release from slavery and exile, the gift of a promised land, deliverance from enemies, the covenant written on stone and on the heart. Within this context, salvation is something that takes place in this life.

The same is true in the New Testament.

In a subjective sense, we are being saved *now* (2 Cor. 2:15), given power (1 Cor. 1:18), victory (1 John 5:4), freedom (Gal. 5:1ff), energy (1 Cor. 12:6), a renewed mind (Rom. 12:2), a new covenant (Heb. 9:15), a new life (1 Cor. 1:30)—in fact, eternal life (John 3:16; Rom. 6:23), starting now.

More importantly, these subjective changes lead to changes in outward behavior (1 Cor. 12–14); they signify an objective change as deep as human nature itself. Because Jesus takes away the sins of the world—both the state of sin as a whole (John 1:29) and individual sins (1 John 2:2)—he repairs man's broken relationship with God and brings us into a state of marital intimacy with God (Rev. 19:9). But why would God do all of this for us? According to John, the Father sends the Son into the world because he loves us (John 3:16–17).

To say that Jesus descended from heaven and then ascended back up to glory is not pious rhetoric. The descent and ascent are like a great sweep of God's arm. In the descent, the Son becomes Emmanuel, "God with us" (Matt. 1:23). According to the Church Fathers, the descent means that the Son leaves heaven to assume complete human nature—indeed, it must be complete, since "whatever is not assumed is not saved." In other words, God willingly took on flesh and came to earth so he could raise us up to himself and fully save us. The higher nature (God) raises up the lower nature (man). Jesus' ascent into heaven takes human nature with Christ back to the Father. According to the *Catechism*:

> This final stage stays closely linked to the first, that is, to his descent from heaven in the Incarnation. Only the one who "came from the Father" can return to the Father: Christ Jesus. "No one has ascended into heaven but he who descended from heaven, the Son of man" (John 3:13). Left to its own natural powers humanity does not have access to the "Father's house," to God's life and happiness. Only Christ can open to man such access that we, his members, might have confidence that we too shall go where he, our Head and our Source, has preceded us.[8]

Or, as Paul says in Ephesians, "He who descended is he who also ascended far above all the heavens, that he might fill all things" (Eph. 4:10).

Peter Speaks through Leo

For 125 years, the positions of two Eastern churches over how to talk about the divinity and humanity of Jesus Christ had hardened. Antioch argued that Jesus has two natures, divine and human, but implied that two natures mean two Persons—in effect, two Sons. Alexandria insisted that there is one Son, of the same nature as the Father and therefore divine, but implied that the humanity is incomplete—Jesus

8. CCC 661; see also ibid., 2795.

has a human body but no human soul. Neither side would budge.

The churches of the East appealed to the Pope. In a long letter called a *tome*, Pope Leo I (440–461) outlined the definitive Tradition of the apostles. He said, in effect, that both Antioch and Alexandria were right—and both were wrong.

The Son, said Leo, is one Person with two natures, but both are complete and intact. "The true God was born in the integral and complete nature of a true human being, entire in what belongs to him, as God, and entire in what belongs to us" as human. The Son's human nature enhances humanity without diminishing deity. This explains how God can be said to die. The Son's existence on this earth is "novel" in that it combines opposites: The eternal becomes temporal, the almighty becomes weak, the God who cannot suffer becomes the man who does. Each nature does what is proper to it. So the human nature can learn, even though the divine nature is omniscient. Jesus is not contradicting himself when he says, on the one hand, that "I and the Father are one" (John 10:30) and on the other, "the Father is greater than I" (John 14:28).[9]

Leo had his letter read into the record of the Council of Chalcedon in 451. When the bishops, hearing this letter, exclaimed, "Peter has spoken through Leo!" they were doing more than recognizing him as the successor of Peter. Leo had deftly cut through the toughest knot in the history of the Creed. Leo's explanation led the Council to affirm the combined Creeds of Nicaea and Constantinople as an accurate statement of the Church's faith in Christ.

---

9. Pope Leo I *Letter to Fabian* 2–4.

"Incarnate of the Virgin Mary, He Became Man, Was Crucified, Died, Was Buried, and Rose Again"

We often hear the word *incarnation*. What does it mean? A carnivore eats flesh; carnal relates to fleshly appetites. *Incarnation* comes from two words: *in* and *caro* (flesh) and means taking on flesh or human form. The Greek version of the Creed dwells lovingly on the mystery of the Incarnation. A more literal translation reads: "took on flesh out of the Holy Spirit and Mary the Virgin, and entered humankind." The Creed is making a twofold point:

- The eternal Son took on temporal "flesh," that is, a mortal, physical nature.
- In taking on this flesh he became a human being.

People reciting the Creed used to kneel briefly at this point. The liturgy still requires us to bow our heads. Why? Primarily because of the stupendous nature of this mystery. The *Catechism* explains:

> Belief in the true Incarnation of the Son of God is the distinctive sign of Christian faith: "By this you know the Spirit of God: every spirit which confesses that Jesus Christ has come in the flesh is of God" (1 John 4:2). Such is the joyous conviction of the Church from her beginning whenever she sings "the mystery of our religion": "He was manifested in the flesh" (1 Tim. 3:16).[10]

It is a great mystery, but the Incarnation is also something we

10. Ibid., 463.

can hear, see, and touch (1 John 1:1–4), though we can never understand it entirely. The Son is not part God and part man but 100 percent God and 100 percent man; Jesus Christ is true God and true man.[11] When Gabriel the archangel spoke to Mary, he used language that reminds us of "the beginning" in Genesis: the Holy Spirit "overshadowed" Mary just as he did the waters in the first creation (Luke 1:35; *cf.* Gen. 1:1–2). A new creation is coming about. When God pitches his tent among us (John 1:14), a response of deep reverence is certainly in order.

How did God enter the human race? The Church has declared the Blessed Virgin Mary, the Mother of Jesus, to be the *Theotokos*, Greek for "God-bearer." Mary is the Mother of God. This certainly doesn't mean she is the mother of the Trinity but rather the Mother of a divine Person: her Son, Jesus. She conceived by the Holy Spirit without sexual union with a man and gave birth while remaining a virgin. Her son took his flesh from her—he received his DNA from her. This is another great mystery, and by declaring Mary the Mother of God, we affirm both his full humanity and his full divinity.

Just because Jesus of Nazareth was God as well as man doesn't mean he looked any different from anyone else. Scripture says that he grew up in his family as is the intended norm (Luke 2:51–52). He experienced the wide range of human emotions, including anger (see Mark 3:5), hunger and thirst (Matt. 4:2; John 19:28), weariness (Matt. 8:24), the desire for companionship (Luke 22:15), and solitude

---

11. Ibid., 464.

(Matt. 14:23)—even sorrow and fear at his impending death (Matt. 26:37). But he was unusual in other respects:

- He was celibate when most men his age were expected to marry, maybe because he was already a bridegroom (Mark 2:19; Rev. 16:9).
- He cast out demons (Luke 11:20).
- He healed the sick (Matt. 8:16–17).
- He raised the dead (John 11:41–44).
- He controlled nature (Luke 8:24).
- He even walked on water (Matt. 14:25–26).

In short, he did everything expected of a messiah (Matt. 11:4–5). He demanded total commitment from his disciples, even above family ties or life itself (Matt. 10:37–39). And he claimed the authority to interpret the covenant (Matt. 5–7) because he himself was the fulfillment of the law (Mark 1:14–15): "Before Abraham was, I am" (John 8:58).

Such claims eventually led to his crucifixion and death. Scripture clearly tells us about these events and their importance for mankind (Rom. 5:6–21; 2 Cor. 5:21). In referring to Jesus' crucifixion and death, however, the Creed is affirming what it has already said about the true humanity of the Son. Strange as it may seem today, some early Christians held to wild speculations about Jesus' death. Some said it was actually God the Father who suffered on the cross (the heresy of *patripassianism*) or that the divinity of Christ separated from his humanity at the last moment (because God cannot die) or that Jesus merely swooned on the cross and recovered after three days. The crucifixion and death of Jesus is a historical event, attested to by non-scriptural documents.

The Creed affirms that the second Person of the Trinity was crucified, actually died, and was buried.

Did Jesus Actually Die on the Cross?

"When they came to Jesus and saw that he was already dead, they did not break his legs. But one of the soldiers pierced his side with a spear, and at once there came out blood and water. He who saw it has borne witness—his testimony is true, and he knows that he tells the truth—that you also may believe. . . . After this Joseph of Arimathea . . . took away his body . . . and bound it in linen cloths with the spices, as is the burial custom of the Jews. Now in the place where he was crucified there was a garden, and in the garden a new tomb where no one had ever been laid. So because . . . the tomb was close at hand, they laid Jesus there" (John 19:33–35, 38, 40–42).

It has been said, "I would accept the Creed if it didn't mention Pontius Pilate, because that attempts to tie the faith to real history." To many the story of Jesus sounds like fantasy, not history. Jesus defied the laws of physics by walking on water, healed the sick, and controlled the weather. He worked miracles, and skeptics can't accept miracles (except for those unexplainable "coincidences" that keep happening). But the Creed affirms that Christianity is true, rooted in history. Some note that the Gospels vary in certain details. Others maintain that the parallels between the life of Jesus and persons and events in the Old Testament appear too neat to be factual, even though history does repeat itself. If Jesus is purely human, some think, then he should be like us in all things—including sin—and so like the Gnostics of the past, some make up romantic legends of Jesus eloping to Persia with Mary Magdalen to raise a family or other such tales. Many such skeptics continue their misinformed search for the "historical Jesus" while they reject the *real* historical Jesus presented in the Gospels.

The Creed is dealing with real history, and in real history Jesus actually did rise from the dead. The New Testament says Jesus *was raised* by the Father (Rom. 10:9) and by the Holy Spirit (Rom. 8:11), but it also says that Jesus *rose* under his own power (Luke 24:34; 1 Thess. 4:14). The whole Trinity was involved. The Resurrection is one of the earliest proclamations of Christ's divinity (Acts 2:24–32). It was a real, physical Resurrection. People could, and did, touch the risen body of Jesus (John 20:27). He ate food (Luke 24:42–43). Paul wrote that over five hundred men had personally seen the risen Jesus (1 Cor. 15:1–8) But Jesus' risen body has properties that belong to a different dimension of physical reality: He can pass through locked doors, veil his identity, and function with all of his wounds clearly visible, including the wound from the spear that lanced his lifeless body. The Resurrection proves the claims of Christianity (Acts 2:36). Paul regards it as so important that Christianity is pointless without it. Jesus is the Living One (Luke 24:5); he is not among the dead, nor can death hold him. His resurrected life is a promise of resurrected life for those who belong to him (1 Cor. 15:20–23).

Is the "Jesus of History" Different from the "Christ of Faith"?

The New Testament insists that the man Jesus of Nazareth is both Lord and Messiah (*Christ* in Greek). Peter was preaching Jesus as Christ within two months of the Resurrection (Acts 2:36), Paul within a few years of it (Acts 9:19–31; 1 Thess. 1:1ff; 2 Thess. 2:1, 14–17). The Gospel writers began writing about thirty years after it (see Mark 1:1). Scripture scholars point out that within a century after the death of Jesus, numerous books were written by people who accepted Jesus as the Messiah. Some were accepted as inspired Scripture. Others (occasionally called "the lost Gospels," though they were never lost) were rejected as not inspired.

Until 200 years ago, people generally assumed that the narratives proclaiming Jesus as the Christ were factual as written. The Enlightenment tried to bring scientific principles to bear on ancient documents, including the Bible, and it was at this time that questions about the "historical Jesus" began to appear.

If anything, questions have multiplied, often with a bias against the supernatural. The "Jesus Seminar," begun in 1985 with about seventy-five scholars, tries to distinguish what Jesus actually did and said from what he did not do or say. It concludes that the "historical Jesus" said less than 20 percent of what the Gospels attribute to him and probably didn't know himself to be divine. Other scholars portray the "historical Jesus" as a revolutionary or a proto-feminist.

Other Scripture scholars observe that the historical Jesus "uncovered" by the Jesus Seminar participants has actually been reconstructed for the modern mind on the basis of slim or nonexistent historical evidence. A Jesus who was nothing more than a wise teacher, who was mistaken about the end of the world, and who didn't actually rise from the dead would render what Christians have believed for centuries illusory.

The fact is that the Gospels do reveal the historical Jesus and are truthful in all they teach and affirm.

"Ascended into Heaven, Seated at the Father's Right Hand, to Come in Glory"

Luke tells the story of the Ascension twice (Luke 24:51; Acts 1:9–11). Mark also mentions it (Mark 16:19). Using parallel events, Luke connects the Ascension with the Resurrection: Two angels ask the disciples why they are staring up into heaven looking for Jesus just as two angels asked the women at the tomb why they sought Jesus among the dead (Luke 24:5). Paul also mentions the Ascension (1 Tim. 3:16) and focuses on its meaning (Eph. 4:8–10).

The glorification of Christ at the right hand of God the Father crowns the resurrection and Ascension. All four Gospels mention the Son at the Father's right hand (e.g., Matt. 26:64; Mark 14:62; Luke 22:69; John 16:28), and the rest of the New Testament refers frequently to his glorification in heaven. In the Bible, the right hand represents power and authority. As a result of his position, the Son can send the Holy Spirit to inaugurate the kingdom of God on earth (John 14:25–26; 16:7–11).

In using the figurative language of ascending and sitting

at the right hand of the Father, the New Testament—and with it, the Creed—turns its attention from history to mystery. The ascension is at the heart of what the eucharistic liturgy calls the "mystery of faith," in which we "profess your Resurrection until you come again." For us the mystery is not limited to the remote past. Nor do we push the Second Coming into the distant future, since the Second Coming of Christ, while not known specifically, is imminent. To God, who is outside space and time, all three events are as one event, part of an eternal present. If Christ is risen, he is not dead but alive. If he is ascended into heaven, he is where he can be present with his disciples "to the close of the age" (Matt. 28:20).

In the Creed, the article on the Son ends with the proclamation that "he will come again in glory to judge the living and the dead, and of his kingdom there will be no end."

Did Jesus Actually Rise from the Dead?

"I delivered to you as of first importance what I also received, that Christ died for our sins in accordance with the scriptures, that he was buried, that he was raised on the third day in accordance with the scriptures, and that he appeared to Cephas, then to the twelve. Then he appeared to more than five hundred brethren at one time, most of whom are still alive, though some have fallen asleep. Then he appeared to James, then to all the apostles. Last of all, as to one untimely born, he appeared also to me" (1 Cor. 15:3–8).

Chapter Five

THE HOLY SPIRIT, BREATH OF LIFE

Pope John XXIII wanted a council, telling the world's bishops that the idea came from the Holy Spirit. When the Second Vatican Council opened in 1962, the Holy Father penned this prayer: "O Holy Spirit, renew your wonders in our time, as though for a new Pentecost." During the Council, schoolchildren all over the world recited that prayer.

A new Pentecost! Immediately we imagine the Upper Room, rushing wind, tongues of fire, miracles, and the birth of the Church. Is the Holy Spirit still alive and active in the world today? Who and what is the Holy Spirit?

"We Believe in the Holy Spirit"

Earlier we noted that the titles Father and Son describe their relationship, not their nature. It is the same with the Spirit: The title describes how he acts rather than what he is. Both the Father and the Son have names but we don't know the Spirit by name—we know him by descriptive words such as Holy Spirit and Comforter. We see the effects that follow him (John 3:8). Because of his "divine self-effacement," we know him only in the movement by which he reveals Christ.[1] It is not that difficult to put faces on the Father and the Son, but it's not so easy to put a face on the third Person of the Trinity.

Without elaboration, the earliest creeds simply state, "We believe in the Holy Spirit." Of course, there are other ways to know about the Spirit—Scripture, the liturgy, the charisms, personal experience, and the teaching of the Church.[2] Still, about 300 years after the Holy Spirit descended in fire, the Church fleshed out the doctrine of the Spirit and his equality with the Father and the Son—primarily because his equality was under attack.

The Spirit and the Dove

On a cool spring morning, you may hear mourning doves cooing. For Solomon, this was the voice of spring, and the call of love: "For lo, the winter is past. . . . The flowers appear on the earth, the time of singing has come, and the voice of the turtledove is heard in our land. . . . O my dove . . . let me see your face, let me hear your voice, for your voice is sweet, and your face is comely" (Song 2:11–12, 14).

Springtime and the dove are ideas that come into play when Jesus is baptized in the Jordan; the Holy Spirit alights on Jesus in the form of a dove (Mark 1:10). The image recalls the Spirit of God hovering over the waters at the beginning of creation (Gen. 1:2). When the dove returns to Noah after the flood, it signals a new creation (Gen. 8:10–12),

1. Ibid., 687.
2. Ibid., 688.

and Peter links this imagery with baptism that saves us and brings the Holy Spirit (1 Pet. 3:21)—a new beginning, a new springtime.

In the form of wind and fire, the Holy Spirit rushes into the Upper Room at Pentecost, bringing a new beginning. Christian art typically portrays a dove descending from heaven and hovering over Mary and the apostles.

"The Lord, the Giver of Life"

The Bible begins with the presence of the Holy Spirit. In the beginning "the Spirit of God" (*ruah Elohim*) was moving over the face of the waters (Gen. 1:2). By his word (which requires breath) and through his Spirit, Yahweh creates—he orders the chaos (Ps. 33:6), and by his breath he transforms lifeless dust into Man—a living soul (Gen. 2:7). Human beings have life because the Spirit of God breathes life into them (Job 33:4; Is. 57:16).

The Spirit of God fills the pages of the Old Testament. Even though the Old Testament doesn't explicitly teach that the Holy Spirit is a divine Person, there are occasional hints of personhood (e.g., Is. 63:10). In the Old Testament the Spirit typically appears as a power or force sent by Yahweh. Of the four "elements"—earth, air, fire, and water—the Spirit is associated with three. Like wind parting the Red Sea (Ex. 14:21) and moving God's chariot (Ezek. 1:4–20), the Spirit also breathes life into a field of dry bones (Ezek. 37:1–14) and is detectible in quiet breezes (1 Kgs. 19:11–12). Like fire, the Spirit guides and protects (Ex. 13:21–22), consumes sacrifices (Gen. 15:17; 1 Kgs. 18:38), purifies the heart (Is. 6:5–7; Mal. 3:2–3), and whisks saints to heaven (2 Kgs. 2:11–13). And, like water flowing out of the temple, the Spirit sustains both trees and fish in the desert (Ezek. 47:1–10).

The Spirit is the holy, subtle, all-powerful, all pervading breath of Yahweh (Wis. 7:22–25). He gives skill to craftsmen (Ex. 31:3), wisdom to the servant of Yahweh (Is. 42:1–4), and bestows charismatic understanding, courage, and fear of the Lord upon messianic kings (Is. 11:1–3). Anointed leaders bequeath a "portion" of the Spirit to their successors (Deut. 34:9; 2 Kgs. 2:9ff), and the Spirit enables Israel's leaders (Mic. 3:8; Zech. 4:6).

The New Testament mentions the Holy Spirit more than 240 times. In one respect, the view of the Holy Spirit in the New Testament resembles that of the Old.

The Spirit is an overwhelming force, driving even Jesus into the wilderness (Mark 1:12). He transports people from place to place, both physically (Acts 8:39) and in visions (Rev. 17:3). He directs and prevents evangelism in some places (Acts 8:29–38; 16:6–7). The Spirit is life-giving Power (Luke 1:35), and his flaming power immerses (baptizes) believers in Spirit (John 1:33) and dramatically changes peoples' lives (Acts 2; 10:44–47).

From Holy Ghost to Holy Spirit

English-speaking Christians used to refer to the third Person of the Trinity as "the Holy Ghost." Many still do. According to the Oxford English Dictionary, *ghost* meant a blast of air or breath, as in "the *ghost* of God's mouth." By the sixteenth century, *ghost* was used to translate the Latin word *spiritus*, as readers of the Protestant King James translation are aware.

But times change, and words shift meaning. *Ghost* lost its connotation of breath or wind and came to mean simply a disembodied spirit such as a departed soul. Thus, the word lost contact with its scriptural meaning. So, even though old hymns and prayers still refer to the Holy Ghost, most modern Bibles in English now speak of the Holy Spirit.

But whereas the Old Testament tends to portray the Spirit of Yahweh as an *it*, the New Testament introduces the Spirit as a *he*. Jesus uses the personal pronoun: He will dwell with you, he will teach you, he will bear witness, he will guide you (John 14:17, 26; 15:26; 16:13). Paul says that the "Spirit *himself*" comes to help us (Rom. 8:26). The Spirit does what only a person can do: He hears and speaks for the Father (John 16:13), speaks both within Christians (Mark 13:11) and to them (Acts 13:2), comforts (Acts 9:31), commands action (Acts 8:29), invites (Rev. 22:17), teaches (John 14:26; 1 Cor. 2:13), and gives gifts as he wills (1 Cor 12:11). A good psychologist, the Spirit knows the mind of God (1 Cor 2:10–11) and probes the human heart (Rom. 8:27). As a Person, the Spirit can also be lied to (Acts 5:3) and grieved (Eph. 4:30).

Jesus calls the Holy Spirit a counselor. The Greek word *Paraclete* means "one called alongside," an intercessor and advocate (John 14:26). The Spirit is a witness to the truth (1 John 5:7–8), testifying to God's forgiving love (John 5:26; Heb. 10:15). The Holy Spirit also acts as a judge to "convince the world concerning sin and righteousness and judgment" (John 16:8).

We participate in God's inner life when the Holy Spirit dwells in us as God dwelling in his temple (1 Cor. 3:16; Eph. 2:22), inhabiting both soul and body (1 Cor. 3:16; 6:19). The Holy Spirit inhabits our prayer, praying within us and for us (Rom. 8:26–27). He causes growth in faith, hope, and love (Rom. 15:13, 30), the moral virtues (2 Cor. 6:6), and the fruit of the Spirit (Gal. 5:22–25). Since God cannot tolerate sin, the Spirit works from within to sanctify us—disciplining us as God's children (2 Thess. 2:13). That is why God eagerly gives the Holy Spirit in super-abundance (Luke 11:13; John 3:34).

"Who Proceeds from the Father and the Son"

Here we gaze into deep waters. As Pope Leo XIII wrote:

> Whosoever then writes or speaks of the Trinity must keep before his eyes the prudent warning of the Angelic Doctor [St. Thomas Aquinas]: "When we speak of the Trinity, we must do so with caution and modesty, for, as St. Augustine saith, nowhere else are more dangerous errors made, or is research more difficult, or discovery more fruitful."[3]

The Creed uses personal pronouns to emphasize the personhood of the Holy Spirit. In his talk on the Holy Spirit in April, 1989, Pope John Paul II said:

---

3. Leo XII, *Holy Spirit* 3.

> Jesus told the apostles: "I will pray the Father, and he will give you another Counselor" (John 14:16), "the Spirit of truth who proceeds from the Father" (John 15:26), "whom the Father will send in my name" (John 14:26). The Holy Spirit is therefore a Person distinct from the Father and from the Son and, at the same time, intimately united with them.

What do we mean by saying the Holy Spirit "proceeds" from the Father? As noted earlier, the Son is "eternally begotten" by the Father. "Begetting" is figurative. Father and Son describe a relationship—the Son comes from the Father through a kind of *begetting*. The divine origin of the Son takes place eternally "inside" God without a beginning and is beyond our efforts to fully comprehend.

It is the same for the Holy Spirit. We do not speak of the Father "begetting" the Spirit, because the relation of Father and Spirit is different from that of Father and Son. So to describe the eternal "origin" of the Holy Spirit we use different terms: the Spirit *proceeds from* or *comes out of* the Father and the Son. Theologians use the language of breathing: The Holy Spirit, the third Person of the Trinity, "spirates" out from the Father and the Son.[4] Three Persons yet one Being, one God. What we know of God is true but not exhaustive. It is impossible for finite creatures to fully comprehend the infinite.

---

4. CCC 246.

Biblical Symbols for the Holy Spirit

The *Catechism* lists eight symbols for the Holy Spirit:

Water: "The symbolism of water signifies the Holy Spirit's action in baptism, since after the invocation of the Holy Spirit it becomes the efficacious sacramental sign of new birth."

Anointing: "In Christian initiation, anointing is the sacramental sign of confirmation, called 'chrismation' in the churches of the East."

Fire: "While water signifies birth and the fruitfulness of life given in the Holy Spirit, fire symbolizes the transforming energy of the Holy Spirit's actions."

Cloud and Light: "In the theophanies of the Old Testament, the cloud, now obscure, now luminous, reveals the living and saving God while veiling the transcendence of his glory." In the New Testament, the Spirit "overshadows" Mary, then Jesus, as his name, nature, and role are revealed.

Seal: A symbol of ownership. "'The Father has set his seal' on Christ and also seals us in him."

Hand: "It is by the apostles' imposition of hands that the Holy Spirit is given."

Finger: "The hymn *Veni Creator Spiritus* invokes the Holy Spirit as the 'finger of the Father's right hand.'" Think of Michelangelo's fresco of God touching lifeless Adam with his finger to imbue life in him.

Dove: "Christian iconography traditionally uses a dove to suggest the Spirit."[5]

---

5. Ibid., 694–701.

This is where the doctrine of the Holy Spirit came under attack. Just when it was settled that the Son is "one in being" with the Father, a group nicknamed "Spirit-Fighters" (essentially Arians) taught that the Holy Spirit was not God. They could agree with the Nicene Creed when it says that "we believe in the Holy Spirit" because it was vague, but they viewed the Spirit as an angel, some sort of creature. St. Athanasius (and others) fought the "Spirit-Fighters," and they disappeared quickly.

Controlling Baser Instincts

The Holy Spirit indwells in you to train you to resist your lower, natural impulses and act more like God. He teaches you to think like God (Rom. 12) and kill everything in you that is sinful and worldly (Col. 3:5–10), because evil and sin are not "natural." If one day you are to live in God's house, you must be prepared for that. And that will take a lifetime of work—by both parties.

Many Eastern Orthodox say that the Spirit proceeds from the Father alone; others maintain that the Spirit proceeds from the Father *through* the Son. The latter is understood by some Catholics and Orthodox alike as equivalent to "from the Father and the Son." The *Catechism* notes that these interpretations are open to each other so long as one does not press them too rigidly.

Then there are the Orthodox who do not have a problem saying that the Spirit proceeds from the Father and the Son but that the Catholic Church simply should not have added the word *filioque* to the Creed—at least not without Orthodox participation in the process. Even some Eastern Orthodox who agree with this position nevertheless do not include the *filioque* in their liturgies. The same is true for some Eastern Catholic Churches.

So does the Spirit proceed from both the Father and the Son? Scripture refers to the "Spirit of the Son" (Gal. 4:6), the "Spirit of Christ" (Rom. 8:9), or the "Spirit of Jesus" (Phil. 1:19),[6] who is sent by the Son (John 16:7). Jesus breathes on the disciples saying, "Receive the Holy Spirit" (John 20:22). Therefore, Church Fathers of both East and West taught that since the Spirit comes *from* the Father *through* the Son, it is appropriate to say that he proceeds from both the Father *and* the Son. Pope Leo I affirmed this as the faith of the Church in 447. In 589, a council of bishops in Toledo, Spain, added "and the Son" (*filioque*) to the Nicene Creed. The expression became part of the Western liturgy.[7] But the Orthodox never adopted it, making the *filioque* a bone of contention between the Catholic and Orthodox churches. Many theologians on both sides fail to see the *filioque* as a justification for continued schism.

The *Catechism* on the Filioque Debate

"At the outset the Eastern tradition expresses the Father's character as first origin of the Spirit. By confessing the Spirit as he 'who proceeds from the Father,' it affirms that he comes from the Father through the Son. The Western tradition

6. Ibid., 245.
7. Ibid., 246–248.

expresses first the consubstantial communion between Father and Son, by saying that the Spirit proceeds from the Father *and* the Son (*filioque*). It says this, 'legitimately and with good reason,' for the eternal order of the divine Persons in their consubstantial communion implies that the Father, as 'the principle without principle,' is the first origin of the Spirit but also that as Father of the only Son, he is, with the Son, the single principle from which the Holy Spirit proceeds. This legitimate complementarity, provided it does not become rigid, does not affect the identity of faith in the reality of the same mystery confessed."[8]

"He Is Adored and Glorified"

None of the earliest creeds refer explicitly to the Holy Spirit as *God*. However, the expanded Nicene Creed calls the Spirit the "Lord," who "with the Father and the Son is adored and glorified." God alone is to be worshiped and glorified; therefore we acknowledge the glory and divinity of the Holy Spirit.

The Creed follows Scripture by placing the Holy Spirit on the same level of being as the Father and the Son.[9] The New Testament is clear: "The Lord is the Spirit" (2 Cor. 3:17); the Spirit is "another Counselor" (John 14:16) who dwells permanently with the disciples. Jesus commands baptism in the name (singular) of the Father and of the Son and of the Holy Spirit (Matt. 28:19). The Holy Spirit's presence assures us of God's' indwelling (1 John 4:13). Paul prays

8. Ibid., 248.
9. Ibid., 685.

that the Corinthians receive "the grace of the Lord Jesus Christ and the love of God and the fellowship of the Holy Spirit" (2 Cor 13:14). Blasphemy is an attack on God, and Jesus warns that blasphemy against the Holy Spirit will not be forgiven (Matt. 12:31–32).

Though the Creed affirmed the Spirit's divinity, Rome removed any doubt. In 382, a synod called by Pope Damasus declared:

> Anyone who denies that the Holy Spirit is to be adored by all creatures just as the Son and the Father [are adored] is a heretic. . . . Anyone who has a correct idea about Father and Son, but not about the Holy Spirit, is a heretic.[10]

So the Spirit is God in the same way the Son is God. The Catechism teaches that the Holy Spirit is "consubstantial with the Father and the Son"[11] and "is truly God."[12] Calling the Holy Spirit "the third Person" of the Trinity does not suggest that he is inferior to the Father or to the Son.

"He Has Spoken through the Prophets"

This statement of the Creed is foundational to all the other statements. If the Holy Spirit hasn't spoken through the prophets, then divine revelation means nothing. But the

---

10. "Tome of Damasus," 306/22–23, in J. Neuner, S.J., and J. Dupuis, S.J., *The Christian Faith in the Doctrinal Documents of the Catholic Church*, 7th ed. (New York: Alba House, 2001), 145–46.
11. CCC 685.
12. Ibid., 689.

opposite also is true: If the Holy Spirit *has* spoken through the prophets, then divine revelation means everything.

In the Creed, the term *prophets* refers primarily to those who wrote the books of Scripture, which unfolds the revelation of God.[13] In this sense, the writers of the Old and New Testaments are prophets. All of Scripture is inspired (breathed) by God (2 Tim. 3:16–17), and Peter calls Scripture Spirit-inspired prophecy (2 Pet. 1:20–21). This is enormously practical, since once we understand that Scripture is God-breathed, we no longer judge its value; rather, we listen to it, believe it, and obey it.

Secondly, prophets include biblical personalities who had a recognized charism of prophecy, such as Elijah, Isaiah, Jeremiah, and many others, including several women, such as Miriam (Ex. 15:20), Deborah (Judg. 4:4), Anna (Luke 2:36), and the daughters of Philip (Acts 21:9). Prophets also include Moses (Deut. 34:10; Acts 3:22), David (Matt. 22:43), John the Baptist (Matt. 21:26), and Jesus himself (Matt. 21:11; Luke 24:19). These prophets of the Bible contributed to the public revelation of the faith—the revelation intended for the Church as a whole.

So, what does a prophet do? Occasionally, the prophet foretells the future (e.g., Is. 7:14 about the birth of Immanuel), but primarily the prophet listens to God, receives his word, and then proclaims it. The true prophet does not invent his message but only speaks God's words. The false prophet speaks out of his own mouth (Jer. 23:30–32). In 1 Corinthians 12–14, Paul says prophecy comes through utterances of wisdom, knowledge, discernment, and even

13. Ibid., 702.

tongues. Prophets must yield to God's charism, and the hearers must evaluate prophecy and act appropriately (1 Thess. 5:20–21). Both must be attentive and obedient to the Spirit.

The *Catechism*, reflecting the Second Vatican Council, recommends all of the charisms:

> Whether extraordinary or simple and humble, charisms are graces of the Holy Spirit that directly or indirectly benefit the Church, ordered as they are to her building up, to the good of men and to the needs of the world.[14]

Pope John XXIII prayed for a new outpouring of the Holy Spirit, a new Pentecost. By calling the Second Vatican Council, Pope John was not longing for the "good old days," but wanted the Spirit unleashed on the modern world. Pope John Paul II said, "the Christian can hold his head high and join in the invocation that the Holy Spirit raises throughout history: 'The Spirit and the Bride say, Come!' "[15] God invites us to drink deeply of his Holy Spirit.

What Is a Charism?

The *Catechism* demonstrates the importance of the charisms, or charismatic gifts, by mentioning the term nearly two dozen times. Charisms fall into two general categories:

1. *Internal* graces given by the Holy Spirit (the "Isaian" charisms).

2. *Outward* expressions of these internal gifts (the "Pauline" charisms).

14. Ibid., 799.

15. John Paul II, general audience of July 3, 1991.

To most Catholics, the Isaian charisms belong to confirmation: wisdom, knowledge, understanding, counsel, fortitude, piety, and fear of the Lord (Is. 11:2–3). But they need to come out. Paul provides partial lists in his letters (for example, see 1 Cor. 12, 14). The *Catechism* refers to these Pauline charisms when it says:

> Charisms are to be accepted with gratitude by the person who receives them and by all members of the Church as well. They are a wonderfully rich grace for the apostolic vitality and for the holiness of the entire body of Christ, *provided they really are genuine gifts of the Holy Spirit and are used in full conformity with authentic promptings of this same Spirit*, that is, in keeping with charity, the true measure of all charisms.
>
> It is in this sense that discernment of charisms is always necessary. No charism is exempt from being referred and submitted to the Church's shepherds. "Their office [is] not indeed to extinguish the Spirit but to test all things and hold fast to what is good," so that all the diverse and complementary charisms work together "for the common good" (empahsis added).[16]

16. Ibid., 800–801.

Chapter Six

A GREAT MYSTERY—THE CHURCH

"It doesn't matter what church you attend as long as you love Jesus."

"Jesus didn't intend to start a Church; it was invented later by Paul."

"I don't go to church because they are full of hypocrites—plus my relationship with God is private."

These are common sentiments about the Church, and differing opinions are as numerous as birds in the air.

The Creed proclaims that the Church exists and can be identified by certain marks. Throughout history divisions have sliced through Christianity. By stating that the Church is **one**, **holy**, **catholic**, and **apostolic**, the Creed cuts through the confusion and sinks deep roots into Scripture, Tradition, and history.

Mentioning the Church was not standard fare in the earliest creeds. Usually, creeds and doctrines are developed when the truth of the faith is challenged. The original Nicene Creed ended with the article on the Holy Spirit. The phrase "holy Church" is, however, found in a creed from A.D. 170, Hyppolytus's third century creed, and the Apostles' Creed of the fourth century. A short Egyptian creed on papyrus referred to "the holy *catholic* Church" and many subsequent creeds followed that wording. To emphasize unity, Cyril of Jerusalem added the word *one*—"*one* holy and catholic Church" (c. 348). In 374, Epiphanius of Salamis, probably in response to disputes over authority, added the word *apostolic*. In 381 the Council of Constantinople expanded the Nicene Creed to read "one, holy, catholic, and apostolic Church." Though descriptions were added over time, the concepts and truths were there and believed from the very beginning.

By adding these qualifiers, what does the Creed profess about the Church?

We Believe in *the* Church

IMAGINE a filthy beggar summoned out from the crowd for exclusive membership in an elegant society. Each of us has been called out of the world to join such a society—the kingdom of God. The Greek word for *church* is *ekklesia*, derived from a verb meaning "to call out." In secular usage, it meant a political assembly of citizens in a democratic city-state. Because biblical authors writing in Greek adapted the secular word to Christian use, some modern scholars argue that its political connotations carry over into the biblical idea of church.

Ekklesia translates two Old Testament Hebrew words for "community": *edah* and *qahal* (Deut. 9:10; 18:16). The *qahal Yahweh* is the "assembly of God," the people of Israel—a particular people chosen and called out by God (Deut. 5:1–22), separate from the nations, and holy as God is holy (Deut. 7:6; 14:2, 21; Lev. 19:2). Yahweh was the king of the rag-tag group of former slaves he had formed into a nation (Ex. 24:3; Ps. 10:16; 47:2). Obeying God made Israel great (Deut. 4:6–8). Moses spoke for God, taught the assembly, and demanded strict obedience to God's law (Deut. 33). The Israelites agreed to obey the Lord (Ex. 19:8; 24:3)—and there was nothing democratic about it.

The Greek word *ekklesia* is also the New Testament word for "Church," and it appears only three times in the Gospels (Matt. 16:18; 18:17). It means what *qahal* does, an assembly of God. In the Gospels there are many images used for the Church. Examples include the vineyard (Matt. 21:33–43), the vine and the branches (John 15:1–5), the shepherd and his flock (John 10), the new Israel with Jesus as the new Moses (Matt. 5–7), the net full of fish (Matt. 4:19; John 21:8), and the house built on rock (Matt. 7:24–25).

Where Do We Get the Word *Church*?

When Latin writers spoke of the Church, they simply imported the Greek word *ekklesia* ("those called out to form a separate society") with a slight change of spelling: *ecclesia*. Modern European languages descended from Latin still retain traces of the Greek. On Sunday, Spaniards go to *la iglesia*, French to *l'*église, and Italians to *la chiesa*. Even the English word *church* comes from Greek—but through a different route. The adjective *kyriake* means something that belongs to the Lord (*kyrios*). With a few changes in pronunciation and spelling, the word passes through German as *kirche*, *kirk* in Scotland, and *church* in England. So the Church and all of its fullness belongs to the Lord.

But it is the image of the kingdom that predominates; it is mentioned more than 100 times in the Gospels. The kingdom begins small but grows very large (Matt. 13:1–43); everyone is invited into it (Matt. 13:47–48; 20:1ff); even tax collectors, prostitutes (Matt. 21:31), the poor, and the humble (Matt. 5:1ff; 19:23). The Church is the realization of God's kingdom on earth:

> The Father's will is "to raise up men to share in his own divine life." He does this by gathering men around his Son Jesus Christ. This gathering is the Church, "on earth the seed and beginning of that kingdom."[1]

In the rest of the New Testament the word *ekklesia* is used more than 110 times. Most often, it refers to a local church that gathered in a home (Rom. 16:3–5) or to all the Christians in a city or region (Acts 9:31). But *ekklesia* often means something larger, as when Paul speaks of "the household of God, which is the church of the living God, the pillar and bulwark of the truth" (1 Tim. 3:15). The Church is the body of Christ. Jesus is "the head over all things for the Church, which is his body, the fullness of him who fills all in all" (Eph. 1:22–23). All the members of this Church are the members of Christ's body whose different organs work together as a single organism (1 Cor 12:24–30).

What spread so quickly in the period described in the New Testament was not a new religion but the Church. Converts flocked to the apostles, who taught them and organized local churches centered around the Eucharist and community prayer (Acts 2:42). To follow Christ apart from the Church

---

1. CCC 541; *cf.* Second Vatican Council, *Lumen Gentium* 2, 5.

was in the Greek sense idiotic, for an *idiot* (a private, unsociable individual) separated himself from teaching, fellowship, and prayer. As persecutions forced emigration from Judea, and as the Church filled with Gentiles, it spread rapidly from Rome to India, forming a network of local churches.

Network is the key word, for interconnection was crucial. Apostolic letters were passed from one local church to another, and it was just such a letter that described the Church as something far more than merely independent and local congregations. In the hymn that opens his letter to the Ephesians, Paul describes the mystery of God's will unfolding in Christ since the beginning of time (Eph. 1:9–10). Working first in and through the Israelite people (Eph. 1:11–12), God has now poured out his Holy Spirit on everyone, establishing Christ as "head over all things for the Church, which is his body, the fullness of him who fills all in all" (Eph. 1:22–23). The death and resurrection of Christ have drawn those who were far off (Gentiles) and those who were near (Jews) into one body, bringing to an end the hostility between them (Eph. 2:11–16). All Christians belong to one household, founded on the apostles and prophets, with Christ as the cornerstone (Eph. 2:19–22). Paul was sent to proclaim this mystery so that even the "principalities and powers" in the unseen world would learn about God's incomprehensible wisdom through the Church (Eph. 3:8–10).

The Church is also more than simply what we see on a Sunday morning. It is one large family—a kingdom that reaches beyond space and time. The Church includes the faithful on earth (called the "Church Militant"). But the Church also includes the saints in heaven (the "Church Triumphant") and the souls being purified in purgatory (the "Church Suffering"). This communion of saints, with Jesus Christ as the head, comprises the Church.

It exists on two levels: the visible and the mystical, or invisible. The Vatican II constitution on the Church, *Lumen Gentium*, emphasizes that the Church is not two separate realities but one:

> The society structured with hierarchical organs and the mystical body of Christ, the visible society and the spiritual community, the earthly Church and the Church endowed with heavenly riches, are not to be thought of as two realities. On the contrary, they form one complex reality that comes together from a human and a divine element.[2]

The Church consists of more than people and buildings. *Lumen Gentium* reminds us that the Church is a mystery planned by the Father from the beginning, and it is through Jesus' death and resurrection that he draws all men to himself. That mystery now continues through the eucharistic liturgy[3] and the Holy Spirit, who dwells in the Church to sanctify and empower it. In its visible unity, the Church reflects the oneness of the Triune God—"a people brought into unity from the unity of the Father, the Son, and the Holy Spirit."[4]

That may explain why in the Creed, the article on the Church follows the articles on the Trinity—the Church is an

2. LG 8.
3. Ibid., 3.
4. St. Cyprian, *De Orat. Dom.* 23.

ongoing work of the Trinity, communicating the Trinity to everyone.[5] At this point, the Creed lists the four main characteristics, or "marks" of the Church.

We Believe in *One* Church

In 1980, David Barrett identified over 20,800 Christian denominations worldwide.[6] By 2000, the number had increased to 33,820 denominations.[7] While even Catholics often refer mistakenly to the Church as a denomination, it is not—it is the *Church*.

Unity is the first distinguishing mark of the Church that Jesus founded. According to Paul, its unity rests on the nature of God and his call:

> There is one body and one Spirit, just as you were called to the one hope that belongs to your call, one Lord, one faith, one baptism, one God and Father of us all, who is above all and through all and in all (Eph. 4:4–6).

In God's plan for his people and the economy of salvation, there is to be *one* Church, undivided. Jesus prayed "for those who believe in me through their word, that they may all be one; even as thou, Father, art in me, and I in thee, that they also may be in us, so that the world may believe that thou

---

5. CCC 747.

6. Daniel G. Reid, ed. *Dictionary of Christianity in America* (Downers Grove, Ill.: InterVarsity Press, 1990), 351.

7. David B. Barrett, *World Christian Encyclopedia* (New York: Oxford University Press, 2001), vol. 1, p. 10.

hast sent me" (John 17:20–21). He also prayed that Christians "become perfectly one" (John 17:23).

Unity among Christians should mirror the unity of God. By this visible unity the "world" should recognize the mission of the one Lord. But the Church's unity must be real and visible or it cannot be seen by the world. Following our Lord, Paul condemned divisions and exhorted communities to strive for unity (e.g., 1 Cor. 1:10; Phil. 1:27–2:3).

From the beginning, the Church developed a common pattern of order, teaching, and worship (1 Cor. 4:17). The earliest Christian communities were governed by a bishop, assisted by deacons and later presbyters (priests). Bishops were responsible for teaching and maintaining sound doctrine (2 Tim. 4:1–5). People entered the Church through a process of initiation culminating with baptism, confirmation, and the Eucharist.[8] The Eucharist was central. Thus, even when the Church was being wracked in the sixteenth century by the division of the Reformation, theologians could still identify the true Church through its three "unities": doctrine, government, and worship.

But if there is only *one* Church and *one* baptism, then what about the 33,820 denominations and all the baptized Christians outside the visible confines of the Catholic Church? In 1964, the Second Vatican Council said that validly baptized persons are joined to Christ and so are in some way joined to the Church, and those elements of sanctification and truth they enjoy impel them "toward Catholic unity."[9] Nevertheless:

---

8. CCC 1229–1232.

9. LG 15; *cf.* CCC 818–819, 838.

> This Church, constituted and organized as a society in the present world, *subsists in* the Catholic Church, which is governed by the successor of Peter and by the bishops in communion with him.[10]

The Rafters' Mutiny

Parable of the Catholic Church by Stephen K. Ray:

The founder of a new country sent his Son to select people to become citizens. A ship was built for the voyage across the ocean to the Celestial City. The ship was equipped with a captain (pope), navigating equipment (Scripture and Tradition), high-tech communications (prayer and the Holy Spirit), food and meals together (eucharistic liturgy), showers (baptism and confession), and every possible supply. The city's glow on the horizon thrilled them all.

Halfway across the ocean the grumbling began. "Who is this captain to tell us what to do? And this food—the same old thing day after day!" Passengers started fighting among themselves, and some decided to jump ship.

So they went below and found wood and rope to build rafts. They gathered supplies and escaped overboard on their rafts. Soon there were over 33,000 little rafts floating at varying distances from the ship. The closer they stayed to the ship (the Catholic Church) the better their chance of reaching the other side; the further away, the less their chance—the other shore. And the good things they have on their rafts—where did they get them?

I didn't jump off the ship. I was born and raised on one

10. LG 8 (emphasis added); *cf.* CCC 816, 820.

of the rafts. After several years I saw a huge shape in the fog and asked my fellow rafters what that was. "You don't want to know!" they whispered. "That's the ship! We avoid the ship."

Well, I did want to know, and after shouting to other rafts and researching log books, I found to my surprise that the founder of the far country had not sent us all out on multiple dangerous rafts but had built a single solid ship. Initially everyone had been on the ship. I knew I had to re-board it.

Once on deck, what should I do about the rafters—should I get the captain to load the canons and declare war on them? No! I couldn't declare war; the founder loved them. I decided to declare love on them and to pray. The people on those rafts were my family and friends. Besides, the rafts were weak with limited provisions; many drifted off to nowhere and many rafters drowned. But others come back to the ship. And even though there are disagreements among shipmates, we are still passengers on one ship waiting to meet our founder in his country. After all, the founder has provided the captain with everything necessary for the ship to weather every storm and adversity.

The Church is certain to arrive safely at its heavenly destination.

The declaration *Dominus Jesus*, published in 2000, explains what "subsists in" means:

> With the expression *subsistit in*, the Second Vatican Council sought to harmonize two doctrinal statements: on the one hand, that the Church of Christ, despite the divisions that exist among Christians, continues

> to exist fully only in the Catholic Church, and on the other hand, that "outside of her structure, many elements can be found of sanctification and truth," that is, in those churches and ecclesial communities that are not yet in full communion with the Catholic Church. But with respect to these, *it needs to be stated that "they derive their efficacy from the very fullness of grace and truth entrusted to the Catholic Church.*[11]

So the Church is *one* in at least two senses. First, there is one Lord who is the sole head of the Church and who founded only one Church, a single people of God. Second, this one Church is a visible society with one government under Peter, the apostles, and their successors, with one deposit of faith and one sacramental worship initiated by baptism and centered on the Eucharist.[12] Whatever effectiveness exists among our separated brethren comes from their baptismal connection with this one Church.

We Believe in One *Holy* Church

How can the Church be holy if it is full of sinners? Shouldn't the Creed say the Church *ought* to be holy, rather than it *is* holy? No. The word *holy* has two meanings: something completely set apart for God[13] and something completely devoid of sin.

---

11. Congregation for the Doctrine of the Faith, *Dominus Iesus* 16 (emphasis added).
12. CCC 815.
13. Ibid., 2810.

Holiness is a mark of God's divinity.[14] It separates him from creation and makes him infinitely good and without sin. No creature is holy as God is holy (1 Sam. 2:2; Is. 6:3). God is love, but Scripture emphasizes his holiness by acclaiming it three times over: "Holy, holy, holy" (Is. 6:3; Rev. 4:8). God demonstrates holiness in many ways, especially through his righteousness (Is. 5:16), his hatred of evil (Ezek. 28:22), and his deliverance of the poor and oppressed (Is. 29:19). What God touches becomes holy by his contact with it (Ex. 3:5); the Holy of Holies and the Ark of the Covenant are holy for that reason (Ex. 26:33; 2 Chr. 35:3). God's selection of Israel makes that people holy because the people now belong to God (Ex. 19:6; Deut. 7:6). Their behavior is meant to reflect that fact (Lev. 19:2).

These themes flow into the New Testament. Jesus, full of the Holy Spirit, is "the holy one of God" (John 6:69). As head of the body, Jesus makes the body holy (Eph. 5:23, 26–27). The *Catechism* speaks of "the whole Church and of each of the faithful, members of his Body, as a bride 'betrothed' to Christ the Lord so as to become but one spirit with him. The Church is the spotless bride of the spotless Lamb."[15] Christ loved the Church and died to sanctify her (Eph. 5:25–26). Christian behavior must reflect that holy relationship (Matt. 5:48; 1 Cor. 6:19–20; 1 Pet. 1:15–16).

The Apostles' Creed calls the Church a "communion of saints," referring to those "called out" to be members of God's holy people. The New Testament characteristically refers to the faithful Christians alive on earth as *saints* (Acts 9:32), but

14. Ibid., 2809.
15. Ibid., 796.

the term also applies to those in heaven.[16] Thus, Paul prays for the Thessalonians to be made holy in preparation for "the coming of our Lord Jesus with all his saints" (1 Thess. 3:13). The term also describes the holiness required of Christians (Rom. 1:7). The saints on earth are united to "the saints in light" (Col. 1:12).

Without holiness no one will ever see the Lord (Heb.12:14), and therefore heaven is peopled exclusively with saints. Through the promises of God we become partakers of the divine nature (2 Pet. 1:4) and are holy because we partake of God's own nature through baptism. Every Christian is called to and capable of achieving personal holiness, which is a result of God's grace and our cooperation as sons (Heb. 12:10). The faithful grow in holiness by the regular practice of the sacraments, submission to God, performance of good works, prayer, self-denial, hatred of sin, service, and virtue. The means and achievement of holiness are within the reach of us all.

The Church exists for holiness.[17] Pope John Paul II observed that the Church's very "structure is totally ordered to the holiness of Christ's members."[18] That means that the hierarchy, the sacraments, the doctrine, and all else exist for one purpose only: to make sinners holy. Scandals, abuses, and sins of even the topmost leaders of the Church can't cloud the fact that the Church is the spotless bride of Christ and exists for the purpose of making saints out of sinners. The Church is both a haven for holy ones and a hospital for sinners.

---

16. Ibid., 1037.
17. Ibid., 824.
18. John Paul II, *Mulieris Dignitatem* 27.

We Believe in One Holy *Catholic* Church

If you visit a strange town and want to attend Mass, you might know where to go by an address, a sign, or even the architecture. The town may have many buildings called "churches" but you would look for a specific one—a church that was *Catholic*.

The word *catholic* comes from two Greek words: *kata* ("according to") and *holon* ("the whole"). Together, they form the adjective *katholikos*, meaning at least three things. First it means whole, entire, with nothing left out. Doctrine is *catholic* when it includes the entire content of the "deposit of faith" as contained in Scripture and Tradition and as handed down by the magisterium. Secondly, it means universal. Originally, *universal* meant "spread throughout the whole world," both in terms of where it is located and the cultures it influences. The Church is *catholic* because it welcomes and embraces all peoples. A possible third meaning of the Greek word is "true" or "authentic" as opposed to false, heretical, or schismatic. This may be what Ignatius of Antioch, writing around A.D. 106, meant when he wrote, "Where Jesus Christ is, there is the catholic Church."[19] The Church Fathers sometimes used all three meanings simultaneously.

Catholicity is a prominent New Testament theme. Jesus said, "I have other sheep that are not of this fold; I must bring them also. . . . So there shall be one flock, one shepherd" (John 10:16). The apostles must "make disciples of all nations, baptizing them . . . [and] teaching them to observe all that I have commanded you" (Matt. 28:19–20). Luke tells

19. Ignatius of Antioch, *Letter to the Smyrnaeans* 8, 2.

how "devout men from every nation under heaven" (Acts 2:5) came into the Church at Pentecost. The gospel Paul preached to the Colossians "in the whole world . . . is bearing fruit and growing" (Col. 1:5–6). He reminded the Ephesians that this catholicity is the point of God's plan to unite all things in Christ (Eph. 1:10). And though the universal Church is manifested through local churches, in Paul's day and beyond they were unified by the same teaching as taught "in all the churches" (1 Cor. 7:17).

The term *catholic* was used as an adjective by Ignatius of Antioch as early as A.D. 106 in his letter to the Smyrnaeans, already quoted. The *Martyrdom of Polycarp*, written about forty-five years later, uses *catholic* three times to mean "universal" and once to mean "authentic" or "true." Cyril of Jerusalem in the fourth century provides an explanation of the word's meaning and recommends that travelers look for a church that is truly catholic.

Cyril of Jerusalem on How to Pick a Church

Explaining why the Church is called Catholic, Cyril of Jerusalem (c. 315–386) played off the Greek adjective *katholikos*, meaning "total" or "universal."

The church is thus called "catholic" because it is spread throughout the inhabited world from one end to the other and because it teaches in its totality *katholikos*—without leaving anything out every doctrine that people need to know relating to things visible and invisible, whether in heaven or earth. It is also called "catholic" because it brings to obedience every sort of person—whether rulers or their subjects,

> the educated and the unlearned. It also makes available a universal *katholikos* remedy and cure to every kind of sin, whether in body or in soul, and contains within itself every kind of virtue. . . .
>
> If you ever have cause to visit a strange town, do not ask simply . . . "Where is the church?" Instead, ask, "Where is the *catholic* church?" This is the distinctive name of this, the holy Church and mother of us all. She is the bride of our Lord Jesus Christ, the only begotten Son of God.[20]

Many denominations today presumptuously alter the Creed to read "one, holy Christian church" to avoid the obvious historical tie to the Catholic Church. According to Kenneth D. Whitehead:

> No major historical entity has ever been called "the Christian Church." This term came into use only fairly recently by people unwilling to concede that the entity still known as the Catholic Church . . . is the Church.[21]

No sooner did the common description *catholic* become popular than it became part of the name. By the time of the Council of Nicaea in 325, *catholic* was already so widely used that the Council formally appended the expression "Catholic and Apostolic Church" to numerous canons. By the late fourth century, Augustine spoke of the *Catholic* (with a capital *C*) Church to distinguish it from heretical sects.

---

20. Cyril of Jerusalem, "18th Catechetical Lecture," 23, 26, in Alister McGrath, *The Christian Theology Reader* (Cambridge, MA: Blackwell Publishers, 1995), section 7.5.

21. Kenneth D. Whitehead, *One, Holy, Catholic, and Apostolic* (San Francisco: Ignatius Press, 2000), 50.

Surprising to some people, the universal Church's proper title is not "the *Roman* Catholic Church." It is simply "the Catholic Church." Vatican II's Decree on Eastern Catholic Churches describes the universal Church as:

> made up of the faithful who are organically united in the Holy Spirit through the same faith, the same sacraments, and the same government and who, combining into various groups held together by a hierarchy, form separate [i.e., distinct] Churches or rites.[22]

There are about twenty individual church traditions, or "rites," within the Catholic Church, only one of which is called Roman or Latin. The others include the Byzantine Catholic Church (Greek), the Chaldean Catholic Church (Iraqi), the Maronite Catholic Church (Lebanese), and so on. Together, all of these comprise "the Catholic Church." The expression "particular church" can apply to these various rites but usually refers to a diocese in the Latin Church or an eparchy, its equivalent in the Eastern Church.

Referring to Jesus' command to take the gospel to all nations in Matthew 28:18–21, reknowned apologist Frank Sheed reminds us:

> Notice first the threefold "all"—all nations, all things, all days. Catholic, we say, means "universal." Examining the word *universal*, we see that it contains two ideas: the idea of all, the idea of one. But all what? All nations, all teachings, all times. So our Lord says. It is not an exaggerated description of the Catholic

---

22. Second Vatican Council, *Orientalium Ecclesiarium* 2.

> Church. Not by the wildest exaggeration could it be advanced as a description of any other.[23]

"We Believe in One Holy Catholic and *Apostolic* Church"

Many Protestant or independent churches have the word *apostolic* in their name: "Grace Apostolic Tabernacle," "Apostolic Gospel Church," or something on that order. But only the Catholic Church (and the non-Catholic Orthodox churches) can truly claim the title *apostolic*. As for the Catholic Church:

- it is founded on the apostles whom Christ sent into the world;
- with the guidance of the Holy Spirit, it must teach the fullness of what the apostles taught; and
- those who have succeeded the apostles are responsible for teaching, sanctifying, and governing the Catholic Church.

Taken together, these three components comprise the *apostolic* character of the Church.[24] Looking at each in turn:

The Church is apostolic because it is built on the apostles. Different metaphors are used to illustrate this truth. The Lord built his Church on Peter, the Rock, and gave him the keys of authority to govern and care for the flock (Matt. 16:18–19; Luke 22:32; John 21:15–17). Paul compares the Church to a house "built upon the foundation of the apostles

---

23. Frank Sheed, *Theology and Sanity* (San Francisco: Ignatius, 1993), 284.
24. CCC 857.

and prophets" (Eph. 2:20). Paul himself is a master builder, laying a foundation for others to build on (1 Cor. 3:10). John compares the Church to a city, the New Jerusalem, whose walls have "twelve foundations, and on them the twelve names of the twelve apostles of the Lamb" (Rev. 21:14). The apostles are not static monoliths but living stones whom Christ sends into the world calling all men to be "built into a spiritual house" (1 Pet. 2:5) or temple.

The Church is apostolic because it preserves and hands on the full deposit of faith, the apostolic Tradition proclaiming Christ.[25] The Church is the pillar (supporting column) and bulwark (foundation or defensive wall) of the truth (1 Tim. 3:15).

Notice the defensive nature of these images. The Church doesn't invent truth or create doctrines, but under the protective guidance of the Holy Spirit supports and defends the written and oral Tradition, handing it on intact from age to age. John Henry Cardinal Newman argued that this "handing on" implies authority to teach and interpret revelation: "A revelation is not given [by God] if there be no authority to decide what it is that is given."[26] That principle explains how the Church can claim the right to preach the gospel to all nations (Matt. 28:19–20), decide an authoritative canon of Scripture, and exercise a teaching authority—the magisterium—to preserve and interpret the revelation it proclaims.

The Church is apostolic because it has always been and continues to be taught, sanctified, and governed by the

---

25. Ibid., 175, 425.

26. John Henry Newman, *An Essay on the Development of Christian Doctrine* II, 2, 12.

successors of the apostles. Jesus appointed the apostles and gave them their mission (Mark 3:14), which was to perpetuate his presence on earth through the sacraments and to teach others what he had taught them. Teaching authority included the authority to correct errors (e.g., Gal. 1:6–9; 1 Tim. 1:3–7). Scripture is clear that the apostles not only had the authority to appoint successors (Acts 14:23; 1 Tim. 4:14) but also that the successors could appoint successors to follow themselves (Titus 1:5ff; 2 Tim. 2:2).

Some Christians ask, "But what is the big deal about apostolic succession?" It is a big deal because it is God's plan to maintain the unity and integrity of Christian truth and worship. Genuine apostles don't send themselves; they are ordained and sent by the Church. God sent the Son and the Son sent the twelve (John 20:21), and they, in turn, send their successors. Knowing who appointed whom is critical to identifying who is genuinely ordained in the apostolic succession, a succession that guarantees the authenticity of apostolic authority and teaching. That's one reason the Church Fathers recited lists of bishops from the apostles onward.

In A.D. 96, Clement of Rome, ordained by Peter himself and later to become pope, wrote:

> Equipped as they were with perfect foreknowledge, [the apostles] appointed the men [bishops] mentioned before, and afterwards laid down a rule once for all to this effect: When these men die, other approved men shall succeed to their sacred ministry.[27] In the writings

---

27. *Clement* 42, 44 in Johannes Quasten, *Patrology* (Westminster, Md.: Christian Classics, 1993), vol. 1, p. 45–46.

> of a traveler named Hegesippus (c. A.D. 175), we have the first recorded use of the term *succession*. He used it while listing the bishops of Corinth and Rome down to his own day to verify correctness of doctrine.[28] In the same vein, Irenaeus in about A.D. 180 enumerates the succession of bishops of Smyrna, where he grew up, and of Rome, concluding: "Therefore we ought to obey only those presbyters who are in the Church, who have their succession from the apostles . . . who with their succession in the episcopate have received the sure gift of the truth according to the pleasure of the Father." He adds that ministers *not* in the line of apostolic succession are either heretics, schismatics, or hypocrites.[29] Irenaeus's argument was a common one in churches of both the East and the West.

The Church has been hierarchical in structure from the start—it is not the "democracy of God." Jesus appointed the twelve for specialized ministry (Matt. 10:1, 5ff) with authority to bind and loose (Matt. 18:18), placing Peter at the head (Matt. 16:19; John 21:15–17). A three-tiered structure took on embryonic form in the New Testament. In Acts, the apostles appoint a group of "deacons" whose main function was to serve (Acts 6:1–4). Paul refers to "overseers" (from which we get our word *bishop*), "presbyters," and deacons in some of his pastoral letters (for example, 1 Tim. 3), and he includes "bishops and deacons" as recipients of his letter to the Philippians.

---

28. Eusebius, *History of the Church* IV, 22, 2.
29. Irenaeus, *Against Heresies* III; IV, 26, 2.

The Importance of the Bishop

Facing execution at the jaws of lions, Bishop Ignatius of Antioch described the three-level hierarchy of the local church and the importance of the bishop:

> All of you follow the bishop as Jesus Christ followed the Father, follow the presbyters as the apostles, and respect the deacons as the commandment of God. Let no man perform anything pertaining to the Church without the bishop. Let that be considered a valid Eucharist over which the bishop presides or one to whom he commits it. Wherever the bishop appears, there let the people be, just as, wherever Christ Jesus is, there is the Catholic Church. It is not permitted to either baptize or hold a love-feast eucharistic liturgy apart from the bishop. But whatever he may approve, that is well-pleasing to God, that everything you do may be sound and valid.[30]

Definitions of roles at this early stage are fluid, but by the time of Clement of Rome and Ignatius of Antioch—that is, closer to the time of Jesus than we are to World War I—roles had begun to solidify into what we know as bishop, presbyter or priest, and deacon. Clement tells the Corinthian church that lay people are "bound by the precept laid down for them,"[31] namely, adherence to the local hierarchy.

Thus, the hierarchy of the Church is not the creation of

30. Ignatius of Antioch, "Letter to the Smyrnaeans" 8, in Henry Bettenson, ed., *Documents of the Christian Church*, 2nd Edition (London: Oxford University Press, 1963), pp. 63–64.

31. Clement, *First Letter to the Corinthians* 40.

a power-hungry elite but is a gift from God. *Lumen Gentium* 4 reminds us that the Holy Spirit bestows both charismatic (1 Cor. 12) and hierarchical gifts (Eph. 4:11–13) on the Church. These gifts are like centrifugal and centripetal planetary forces: both are complementary and both are necessary for the system to work. If centrifugal charismatic gifts are not balanced by the centripetal hierarchical gifts, they can explode into ecclesiastical space-dust. By the same token, hierarchical gifts tend to gravitate inward; if they aren't balanced by the centrifugal charismatic gifts, they can implode into a black hole of legalism. But both are gifts of the Holy Spirit for the Church.[32] As long as they work together, the Church maintains a stable orbit around the Son.

The *Catechism* concludes: "The Church is ultimately *one, holy, catholic and apostolic* in her deepest and ultimate identity, because it is in her that 'the kingdom of heaven,' the 'reign of God' already exists and will be fulfilled at the end of time."[33] These "marks" of the kingdom lead the Church into the maturity of the "complete man," the person of Christ as we see him at the end of time. There is *one* people of God, "the *holy* city Jerusalem coming down out of heaven from God, *catholic* in its population, founded on the twelve *apostles* of the Lamb." This picture points forward to the end of time and the return of the Lamb.

---

32. CCC 798, 951.
33. Ibid., 865.

Chapter Seven

OUR WEIGHT OF GLORY

Matthew tells the puzzling story of an earthquake that occurred at Jesus' death. "The earth shook, and the rocks were split; the tombs also were opened, and many bodies of the saints who had fallen asleep were raised, and coming out of the tombs after his Resurrection they went into the holy city and appeared to many" (Matt. 27:51–53).

Legend? Hollywood special effects? An omen? Earthquakes are common in Israel and were often perceived as God stomping his foot, so to speak (Ps. 18:7). When God appears, the mountains quake and the earth melts (Nah. 1:5). Amos prophesied about a future earthquake (Amos 1:1) so terrible that centuries later Zechariah referred to it predicting the Day of the Lord, when "the Lord your God will come, and all the holy ones with him" (Zech. 14:5). Though earthquakes may be good signs at times (Hag. 2:6–7), they usually inspire dread (Is. 13:6; Amos 5:18; Joel 1:15) and fear of punishment (Obad. 1:15). But they also provide a chance for repentance (Mal. 4:5–6). The Day of the Lord is a day of doom and judgment. On the Last Day the dead will arise either to eternal glory or to eternal horror and disgrace (Dan. 12:2; John 5:28–29).

Matthew described the earthquake to show how God

used it to emphasize the cosmic and eternal significance of the death and resurrection of Jesus (Matt. 27:54; 28:2). The Day of the Lord has begun. Note that the first quake opened graves on Good Friday, but their occupants came out and entered Jerusalem three days later—*after* the Resurrection. Jesus' death and resurrection are one earth-shattering event, shaking the kingdom of death and beginning the Last Age.

The last articles of the Creed refer to the four last things: death, judgment, heaven, and hell. These loom large and imposing. We cannot avoid it; the end will come.

The Four Last Things

"Not to admit, therefore, to these four ends of death, judgment, heaven, and hell, the Catholic believer can be neither Catholic nor believing, because here is the central deposit from which all else is derived; here begins the vibrant and unending narrative of the Christian life, the long journey home to God. In order to function at even the most minimal level of Christian awareness, one has got to face the questions that, in the phrase of French mathematician and Catholic apologist Blaise Pascal, take us by the throat:

" 'How am I to die a good and holy death? How am I to meet judgment before God? How am I to avoid hell? How am I to obtain heaven? When everything depends on how one squares off before these questions, and none are at liberty not to face each searing encounter, then the key element in the whole process becomes, in a word, hope. Without doubt, the theological virtue of hope is the defining experience when facing the End.' "[1]

Judge of the Living, Judge of the Dead

Both the Apostles' Creed and the Nicene Creed repeat Jesus' promise that he "will come again to judge the living and the dead." The Nicene Creed adds that Jesus will come "in glory," and his "kingdom will have no end."

Jesus will come "in the glory of his Father with the holy angels" (Mark 8:38). Using imagery reminiscent of Amos, Joel, and Isaiah, Jesus speaks of a kind of "sky-quake" when the "powers of the heavens will be shaken" and the Son of man will appear in heaven and all mankind will see "the Son of man coming on the clouds of heaven with power and great glory" to inaugurate the Day of the Lord (Matt. 24:29–30). The "judgment of the nations" in Matthew 25 begins with the same vision of the Son of man coming "in his glory, and all the angels with him." Jesus alluded to Daniel's vision of a kingdom given to "one like a son of man" coming "with the clouds of heaven" (Dan. 7:13) when he said of himself, "I tell you, hereafter you will see the Son of man seated at the right hand of Power, and coming on the clouds of heaven" (Matt. 26:64). This claim expedited his execution. After rising from the dead he passed through the clouds and entered into his glory (Luke 24:26; Acts 1:9).

But what will the Second Coming of Christ accomplish that the first did not?

---

1. Regis Martin, *The Last Things: Death, Judgment, Heaven, Hell* (San Francisco: Ignatius Press, 1998), p. 83.

Through his first coming—his birth, death, resurrection, and ascension—Jesus revealed himself as the promised Messiah, Lord over sin and death, and the Savior of mankind. His death on the cross delivered the human race from a state of enmity with God, opening the door for adoption into God's family; his Resurrection from the dead offered the hope of our own resurrection. In his Second Coming, Jesus is the judge: "The Son of man is to come with his angels in the glory of his Father, and then he will repay every man for what he has done" (Matt. 16:27). Several important points flow from this passage:

First, Jesus' Second Coming is for *judgment*.[2] The role of any judge is to render an impartial verdict based on objective criteria. The criterion just given by Matthew is *conduct*: the Son of man will repay each one according to his deeds. In Matthew 25, deeds are good or evil actions.

In short, we are judged by our acts of love or failure to love. But we are also judged on acts of faith or its neglect. For example, Jesus warns that "every one who acknowledges me before men, the Son of man also will acknowledge before the angels of God; but he who denies me before men will be denied before the angels of God" (Luke 12:8–9).

Second, Jesus comes the second time for judgment as a *human being*, the Son of man. Even though fully God, he judges in his humanity. Pope John Paul II noted, "The divine power to judge each and every person belongs to the Son of man. The classical text of Matthew's Gospel [chapter 25] emphasizes the fact that Christ exercises this power not only

2. Ibid., 1040.

as God the Son but also as man."[3] Our moral lives affect our relationships with God but also with our fellow man. Jesus identifies himself with mankind: By serving or failing to serve "the least of these my brethren" (Matt. 25:40), we serve or fail to serve Jesus himself.

Third, Jesus' coming "in the glory of the Father" means that he comes with the Father's *power and authority*. "As the Father raises the dead and gives them life, so also the Son gives life to whom he will. The Father judges no one, but has given all judgment to the Son. . . . The Father . . . has given him authority to execute judgment, because he is the Son of man" (John 5:21–22, 26–27). This power to judge is universal: It extends to "the nations" and to the individual—the Son of Man "will repay each one" (Matt. 16:27). Fourth, judgment is part of Jesus' mission of *salvation*. John Paul II said:

> The scope of the judgment is the full participation in the divine life as the final gift made to man—the definitive fulfillment of his eternal vocation. . . . From the very beginning the order of justice has been inscribed in the order of grace. The final judgment is to be the definitive confirmation of this bond.[4]

Jesus himself said that he came that we might have life and have it abundantly (John 10:10). He came not to condemn the world but to save it (John 3:17).

Obviously, we can't take Jesus' mercy for granted. He

3. John Paul II, "Jesus Christ Has the Power to Judge," September 30, 1987.
4. Ibid.

speaks often of eternal punishment and warns that many choose the way of death because it is easy (Matt. 7:13). However, condemnation is not the focus of judgment. Its purpose is justice and salvation, so that "the righteous will shine like the sun in the kingdom of their Father" (Matt. 13:43). Again, John Paul II said: "As is evident from the parable of the talents (Matt. 25:14–30), the measure of judgment will be the cooperation with the gift received from God, cooperation with grace or its rejection."[5]

The judgment of the dead, therefore, will be a kind of ratification of the person's choices in life and the state of their soul at the moment of death.[6] "And just as it is appointed for men to die once, and after that comes judgment, so Christ, having been offered once to bear the sins of many, will appear a second time, not to deal with sin but to save those who are eagerly waiting for him" (Heb. 9:27–28). The Second Coming will be a time of revelation—of horror and disgrace for those who choose it and an eternal weight of glory for those who choose it (Dan. 12:1–3; John 5:29). For the latter, all of creation will join them in glory (Rom. 8:19) since the Christian promise is for a new heaven *and* a new earth (2 Pet. 3:13).

But what about the judgment of the living?

Human behavior—that is, deliberate, intended, *moral* conduct—starts from either within human nature (what Paul calls the "flesh") or the Holy Spirit (what Paul calls the "spiritual man"), or some blending of the two. Our moral and spiritual lives are so tightly intertwined that one always affects

---

5. Ibid.
6. CCC 1021–22.

the other, for better or for worse. A moral choice is a spiritual choice, and a spiritual choice is a moral one.

The judgment of the living begins with these choices, and the pending verdict hangs on the choices themselves and the fruit they bear. When our conduct is marked by hankering for or engaging in "fornication, impurity, licentiousness, idolatry, sorcery, enmity, strife, jealousy, anger, selfishness, dissension, party spirit, envy, drunkenness, carousing, and the like" (Gal. 5:19–21), we are dominated by "the desires of the flesh"—and thus heading for spiritual death. When our conduct is marked by "love, joy, peace, patience, kindness, goodness, faithfulness, gentleness, self-control" (Gal. 5:21–23; Paul's Greek text suggests control of one's sensual desires), we are cooperating with the Spirit and are headed toward eternal life.

There is a bottom line. If our conduct stays "in the flesh," we cannot please God (Rom. 8:8), but if we live "in the Spirit" we have life and peace (Rom. 8:6).

A healthy spiritual life means an active, personal relationship with the divine Persons of the Trinity, which removes any fear of judgment (1 John 4:18). Judgment is a work of the Holy Spirit within us, convicting us of sin (John 16:8–11)—especially those sins we hide from ourselves. Judgment begins with members of God's household (1 Pet. 4:17), who *want* that judgment to begin now rather than later—a desire reflected in the Psalms.

Since the Lord knows him even in the womb, the Psalmist invites God to probe him and know his thoughts (Ps. 139:15, 23). God sees our hearts and knows all of our wrongdoing, since nothing is hidden from him (Ps. 69:5). Wanting to grow spiritually, the Psalmist pleads with God to reveal to him his most secret faults and preserve him from presuming on God's grace (Ps. 19:12–13). Judgment leads us to repentance, and repentance to conversion[7] and a fuller participation in the death and resurrection of Christ, which is what the Christian life is all about.[8]

"We Confess One Baptism for the Forgiveness of Sins"

Peter asked Jesus how often he should forgive a brother who sins against him. In reply, Jesus told a story of a king whose servant owed him 10,000 talents. Because the servant couldn't pay, the king forgave the debt. The pardoned servant found a fellow servant who owed him 100 denarii. When his fellow couldn't pay, the man jailed the servant until the debt was paid off. When the king found out, he was angry and threw the first servant into jail until his original debt was paid in full. Jesus concludes by warning us that the heavenly Father will do the same to us if we do not forgive our brothers from the heart (Matt 18:21–35).

We can better understand the parable if we put the amounts owed into modern currency. The second servant would have owed the first servant about $6,500, whereas the first servant would have owed the master about $15 billion. Jesus demonstrated how small a thing it is for us to forgive our neighbor compared to the magnitude of what he, as the master, has forgiven us.

Luke's version of the Our Father says, "Forgive us our sins"

7. Ibid., 1041.
8. Ibid., 1002.

(Luke 11:4); Matthew's calls them "debts" (Matt. 6:12). By doing wrong to someone, we incur a debt—we owe something. Debt creates an imbalance of justice that must be set right again by repaying the debt. "Getting even" through retaliation never restores the balance of justice. It perpetuates the imbalance on both sides, creating a downward spiral of debt and wrong. The only solution is to forgive the debt as if it never existed. Precisely as God has done for us.

Forgiveness of sins is a two-sided coin. "Heads" is the responsibility of the guilty person to seek forgiveness, since guilt can paralyze his body and soul (Luke 5:18–25) and resentment can destroy the community (Gal. 5:15). In the Christian community, love and forgiveness are so important that Jesus urges his disciples, "If you are offering your gift at the altar, and there remember that your brother has something against you, leave your gift there before the altar and go; first be reconciled to your brother, and then come and offer your gift" (Matt. 5:23–24).

The "tails" side of the coin is the responsibility of the person wronged to extend forgiveness. Jesus demands that we forgive "seventy times seven" (Matt. 18:22)—that is to say in the parlance of the time, without restriction—not only the brother who sins against us, but even our enemies (Matt. 5:38–45), including those who refuse to ask forgiveness:

> It is . . . 'in the depths of the heart,' that everything is bound and loosed. It is not in our power not to feel or to forget, an offense, but the heart that offers itself to the Holy Spirit turns injury into compassion and

> purifies the memory in transforming the hurt into intercession.[9]

If we want the coin, we have to take *both* sides. When we seek forgiveness from God, we must forgive others in the same measure. Jesus warns that we cannot be forgiven if we do not forgive (Matt. 6:14–15; Luke 6:36–38). We ask God to "forgive us our trespasses as we forgive those who trespass against us." In effect, we ask God not to forgive us *unless* we forgive others.

> The Apostles' Creed associates faith in the forgiveness of sins not only with faith in the Holy Spirit but also with faith in the Church and in the communion of saints. It was when he gave the Holy Spirit to his apostles that the risen Christ conferred on them his own divine power to forgive sins: "Receive the Holy Spirit. If you forgive the sins of any, they are forgiven; if you retain the sins of any, they are retained" (John 20:26).[10]

The Church's power to forgive sins depends on its union with Christ and is founded on the finished work of Jesus and his merits.[11] Forgiveness was purchased by his blood (1 Pet. 1:18–19); his merits achieve our salvation (1 John 1:7). Christ has reconciled the world to God, but this reconciliation must be communicated to mankind through the Church (2 Cor. 5:18–19).

---

9. Ibid., 2843.
10. Ibid., 976.
11. Ibid., 2020.

How Do I Forgive Thee? Let Me Count the Ways . . .

The forgiveness of sins is dependent on the work and merits of Jesus Christ. Only God can forgive sin,[12] but he has entrusted or delegated that authority and ministry to men (John 20:23). Although the sacrament of reconciliation is necessary for the forgiveness of mortal (that is, grave) sins,[13] God provides the Church with numerous remedies and means of forgiveness for venial (that is, lesser) sins.[14] In ascending order of importance, they include:

- the exercise of charity and the virtues (Prov. 16:6)
- reading Sacred Scripture, prayer, sincere worship, and devotion[15]
- reception of the sacraments,[16] particularly baptism,[17] which removes original sin and all personal sins committed up to that point[18]
- sincere repentance and acts of contrition before God; for example, during the Penitential Rite at Mass (Luke 18:13–14; 1 John 1:9)
- the intercession of the saints[19]
- reception of the Eucharist[20]
- the sacrament of reconciliation[21]

12. Ibid., 1441.
13. Ibid., 1456.
14. Ibid., 827, 1434.
15. Ibid., 1437.
16. Ibid., 2839.
17. Ibid., 977f.
18. Ibid., 1279.
19. Ibid., 1434.
20. Ibid., 1366, 1393–1395.
21. Ibid., 1458, 1856.

Both canon law[22] and the Catechism[23] recommend the sacrament of reconciliation as superior to other means because of the graces it provides.

Baptism frees people from sin (Mark 16:16; Acts 2:38). But according to the *Roman Catechism*, a predecessor to the current one:

> If the Church has the power to forgive sins, then baptism cannot be its only means of using the keys of the kingdom of heaven received from Jesus Christ. The Church must be able to forgive all penitents their offenses, even if they should sin until the last moment of their lives.[24]

The forgiveness of sins is woven tightly into the very fabric of the Church. Indeed, the Church *exists* to reconcile sinners to God through the forgiveness of sins.

"We Look Forward to the Resurrection of the Dead and the Life of the World to Come"

Ever wonder what the difference is between a *cemetery* and a *necropolis*? After all, both are burial grounds. The distinction: A *necropolis* is a "city of the dead," a pagan burial place, while *cemetery* comes from a Greek word meaning something like "dormitory," that is, a sleeping-room.

22. Ibid., 988.
23. Ibid., 1458.
24. *Roman Catechism* I, 11, 4.

Early Christians understood death as "falling asleep" (Acts 7:60; 1 Thess. 4:13). Thus the catacombs were called "sleeping chambers." Christians did not "bury" their dead; they "deposited" them. What is deposited is expected to be withdrawn someday, like cash from a bank. For Christians, death is not the end of life but its beginning. In fact, the *Roman Martyrology* (a book of martyrs' stories) lists the day of a martyr's death as his birthday. To the Christian mind, God is not a God of the dead but of the living, for all are alive to him (Luke 20:38). In St. Sebastian's Catacombs in Rome, one wall is covered with graffiti including such words as "Peter and Paul, pray for us!"

Do Catholics Believe in the Rapture?

In the mid-1800s in Scotland, a new teaching arose among many non-Catholics. Commonly known as "the Rapture," it subsequently made its way to America through annotations in the *Scofield Reference Bible*. This teaching claims that Christ will secretly reappear *before* the Last Day—before the Second Coming—to snatch believers and take them to heaven. But in the context of biblical theology and in light of the constant teaching of the Church, "the Rapture" is a novelty—a newly invented doctrine.

Unfortunately it has caused much confusion among some Christians. Scripture teaches that the Second Coming will be preceded by a time of great trouble and persecution of God's people (2 Thess. 2:1–4). This period is often called the tribulation. There is great debate among non-Catholics as to whether there is such a thing as the so-called "Rapture" and, if so, if it will occur before, during, or after the tribulation.

The Catholic Church holds, and has always held, that the Second Coming of Christ, the Last Day, will occur after the tribulation, the time of upheaval. The Church has always taught that there would be two comings of Christ: the first as the Suffering Servant, which culminated in his Ascension, and the second as the Victorious Lord.[25] But it rejects the idea of a secret return in between the two. What the Church has always taught about the end times and the return of Christ is contained in sections 673–677 of the *Catechism*.

Many people spend much time looking for signs in the heavens and in the headlines. This is especially true of Premillenialists, who anxiously await the tribulation because they maintain it will inaugurate the Rapture and the millennium (the 1,000-year reign of Christ). With respect to the resurrection on the Last Day, Catholics believe that the dead in Christ will be raised and assumed into heaven along with those who are alive and remain on the earth. But they reject the *Rapture* inasmuch as it is false teaching.

Peter writes:

> But do not ignore this one fact, beloved, that with the Lord one day is as a thousand years, and a thousand years as one day. The Lord is not slow about his promise as some count slowness. . . . Since all these things are thus to be dissolved, what sort of persons ought you to be in lives of holiness and godliness, waiting for and hastening the coming of the day of God, because of

25. CCC 2612.

which the heavens will be kindled and dissolved, and the elements will melt with fire! But according to his promise we wait for new heavens and a new earth in which righteousness dwells. Therefore, beloved, since you wait for these, be zealous to be found by him without spot or blemish, and at peace (2 Pet. 3:8–9, 11–14).

The doctrine that the dead will rise again is older than Christianity. Well before the time of Christ, the prophet Daniel mentioned the resurrection saying, "At that time your people shall be delivered, every one whose name shall be found written in the book. And many of those who sleep in the dust of the earth shall awake, some to everlasting life, and some to shame and everlasting contempt" (Dan. 12:1–2). Ezekiel tells of dry bones taking on flesh and coming to life again (Ezek. 37:1–14).

The Pharisees and other Jews during Jesus' time believed in the resurrection of the dead (John 11:24; Acts 23:8), and Paul's letters, most probably written before the Gospels, clearly proclaim a resurrection to life for those who "have fallen asleep in Christ" (1 Cor. 15:18). Paul's earliest letter, written to the Thessalonians around A.D. 50, assures believers that:

> The Lord himself will descend from heaven with a cry of command, with the archangel's call, and with the sound of the trumpet of God. And the dead in Christ will rise first; then we who are alive, who are left, shall be caught up together with them in the clouds to meet

> the Lord in the air; and so we shall always be with the Lord" (1 Thess. 4:16–17).

Later, Paul told the Romans that if we are baptized into Christ's death, like him we will rise to life (Rom. 6:5). Those baptized into Christ are new creations (2 Cor. 5:17); he who raised Jesus from the dead will also raise us (2 Cor. 4:14). Paul desires to know (experience) the power of Jesus' Resurrection and, through imitating his suffering, gain a like resurrection from the dead (Phil. 3:10–11); for "our commonwealth is in heaven, and from it we await a Savior, the Lord Jesus Christ, who will change our lowly body to be like his glorious body" (Phil. 3:20–21). Paul's most extensive teaching on the resurrection of the dead is in 1 Corinthians 15, where he is explicit that it is a *physical* resurrection. In the words of the Apostles' Creed, we await the resurrection of the *body*.

But what is *resurrection*? Is it simply a dead person restored to a previous kind of earthly life? If so, then it's only a temporary state, for even those whom Jesus raised from the dead, such as Lazarus, died again. Or is resurrection the recomposition of the original atoms and molecules to reshape the decayed body? If so, there would not be enough atoms to go around for all the bodies to be raised—English scholar C. S. Lewis, in his book *Miracles*, says we live in "second-hand bodies" with atoms acquired from other bodies. One's body completely replaces all of its cells every seven years, even though the person remains the same throughout life. Resurrection of the body involves a new nature being constructed out of the old one. It is a "new heaven and a new earth," a blend of spiritual and physical. "By teaching the resurrection of the body," Lewis said, Christianity "teaches that heaven is not merely a state of spirit but a state of the body as well—and therefore a state of nature as a whole."[26]

"But there is more. Jesus links faith in the Resurrection to his own person: 'I am the Resurrection and the life' (John 11:25). It is Jesus himself who on the last day will raise up those who have believed in him, who have eaten his body and drunk his blood."[27] The dead rise in Christ with a body that has the same characteristics as his.[28] Scripture affirms that "when [God] appears we shall be like him, for we shall see him as he is" (1 John 3:2). Jesus' resurrected body was physical: unlike a mere spirit, he could eat (Luke 24:41–43), and the wounds of the crucifixion were still visible (Luke 24:39; John 20:27). Paul wrote, "What is sown is perishable, what is raised is imperishable. It is sown in dishonor, it is raised in glory. It is sown in weakness, it is raised in power. It is sown a physical body, it is raised a spiritual body" (1 Cor. 15:42–44). The life that follows resurrection is eternal life, "the ultimate end and fulfillment of the deepest human longings, the state of supreme, definitive happiness."[29] It is a body no longer subject to sin and death (1 Cor. 15:50–57).

The *Catechism* explains:

> Because of his transcendence, God cannot be seen as he is, unless he himself opens up his mystery to man's immediate contemplation and gives him the capacity

---

26. C. S. Lewis, *Miracles* (San Francisco: HarperSanFrancisco, 2001), 167.
27. CCC 994.
28. Ibid., 999.
29. Ibid., 1024.

> for it. The Church calls this contemplation of God in his heavenly glory "the beatific vision."[30]

That beatific vision is not a static experience like staring at a view from a mountain peak. Rather, it is the thrill of an ongoing process of discovery, of—in Lewis's phrase in his book *The Last Battle*—exploring "higher up and farther in." Ultimately, the beatific vision is a living, dynamic experience of a person, of one who himself passed through death and rose into a new creation. Heaven is the finite reveling in the infinite; the limited creature fully loving and exploring the infinite Creator with all his infinite wonders. Heaven will be a fully engrossing adventure and love affair with God.

An earthquake shook the earth when Jesus rose from the dead. An earthquake was nature's appropriate response to such a cataclysmic event—and that was just one grave. Lewis reminds us that the word *nature* originates from a Latin future participle meaning "about to be born." Jesus is the firstborn of the new nature. The cosmos is in labor until then (Rom. 8:22–24). We wait for the "world to come," and when that world does finally come, the whole cosmos will quake, as every grave opens and the dead rise to eternal life.

---

30. Ibid., 1028.

Chapter Eight

SOME COMMON OBJECTIONS TO THE CREED

Objection: Other religions do without creeds; why should Christianity be the only major religion to require one?

It would be more accurate to say that Christianity finds the Creed useful in several respects. Short formulas summarizing the faith were used to prepare catechumens for baptism. Later, they were arranged into creeds that were easy to teach, memorize, and recite. The Creed is still useful for:

- catechesis, as the structure of the *Catechism* demonstrates,
- explaining and defending the faith, for when false teachings arose, the creeds were developed to summarize the essentials of Christian belief, and
- refuting errors, for by reciting the Creed, even illiterate Christians could explain the faith and, in the process, foster unity, because having a common confession provided a foundation for one faith, a unity of belief, and conduct.

Objection: Since the Bible contains the very words of God, the existence of a formal creed is unnecessary.

There are many reasons a formal creed is helpful even though the Bible is the written and inspired word of God.

First, the Bible is not structured to be an easy-to-use Church manual or theological textbook. Not everything in the Bible is easy to understand (2 Pet. 3:15–16). We know also that the Bible does not stand alone; God's word is contained not only in the Bible but in Tradition as well.[1]

Second, the word *Bible* is actually a plural noun in Greek meaning "books," referring to a small library. Our system of dividing the Bible into books, and the books into chapters and verses, was not developed until centuries after the Bible was compiled. (Verse divisions were not inserted until 1551.) The Bible contains many kinds of literature: laws, history, poetry, proverbs, prayers, personal letters, prophecies, and more. Understanding its content and history are crucial to interpreting its meaning.

Third, not everything Christians must believe is stated clearly or explicitly in the Bible. For example, John 10:30—"I and the Father are one"—has been used to argue both for and against the Trinity. The same term or phrase in one part of the Bible may be used differently in another part of the Bible. For example, the expression "son of God" means one thing in the Psalms and something very different in the Gospels. The difficulty of interpreting Scripture and the confusion among non-Catholics demonstrates the need for the Creed and the teaching of the Church.

All in all, the Creed summarizes what Christians must believe by distilling the essential truths into a simple, usable form. The Creed supplements the Bible; it does not supplant it.

---

1. Ibid., 80–81.

Objection: Since what is true for one person is not necessarily true for everyone, it is repugnant to the modern mind to require belief in absolute statements of faith.

Modern men often attempt to deny absolute truth. But whether they like it or not, everyone lives in a real world with objective, absolute truth. Everyone balances their checkbook with the assumption that two plus two is always four; everyone lives within the laws of gravity, and anyone who is lied to or slapped in the face considers it morally wrong. It is obvious that absolute truth imposes itself on us. The Church proclaims the objective truth of reality, including the tenets of our faith as revealed by God himself.

The above objection also confuses personal preferences with objective truth. The modern mind may prefer a vegetarian to a carnivorous diet, urban to rural living, or democracy to absolute monarchy. But no sane mind would believe that human beings can live long without food or shelter of any sort or in a state of perpetual warfare. Certain things are true regardless of preferences, and they govern what we believe and how we conduct our lives. The Creed states that certain things are objectively true. They are not negotiable.

A club, a corporation, or a country has some kind of charter that identifies its goals and regulates the conduct of its members, employees, or citizens. Anyone wanting to join one of these groups must know what the charter contains and be willing to abide by it. If he finds the charter "repugnant," then he should not join the group. The *Catechism* points out that the faith of the Church exists before any of us does and that the Church invites us when joining her to subscribe to that faith.[2] The faith and teachings of the Church are its charter containing its truth, goals and way of life. Church members are required to accept the faith because the faith is true. No one should join the Church until he is ready to accept its invitation and personally subscribe to its faith and teachings.

Objection: The Creed should not be closed but should be a living document that changes to reflect various times and cultures.

Times, cultures, customs, and languages change—but human beings do not essentially change. The ways that good and evil present themselves have changed over the centuries, but human responses to good and evil have not. People in high-technology Western cultures murder as readily and for the same reasons Cain did eons ago. In the West we respond to love and forgiveness just as Mary Magdalen did in the East two thousand years ago. The Creed does not address issues that change over time or culture; it addresses things of permanence. Means of expression may vary culturally, but the substance of the content does not.

To call a document "living" often means that it is open to constant change, fluctuating with social and other currents. In this sense, we cannot call the Creed "living." However, in a different sense, the Creed is "living" because it contains the heart of God's truth and continues to inspire through the ages. The Creed can also be considered living because we are still discovering the depths of what it contains. For example,

2. Ibid., 160, 1124.

movements within the Church are prompting further investigation of the nature and activity of the Holy Spirit, and the doctrine concerning the resurrection of the dead remains a source of endless fascination.

Objection: Modern science has rendered the Christian faith obsolete. Nineteenth-century German philosopher Friedrich Nietzsche said that Christians believe in a fantasy world.

Not only has the Christian faith not been demolished by scientific evidence, but it shows signs of vitality and resurgence in many parts of the world with more living members than at any time in history.

Even science requires faith—indeed, the entire scientific *method* requires confidence in the credibility of the ways it reaches conclusions and those results. Also, the scientific method imposes strict limits on itself. It needs to measure, quantify, and experiment in a repeatable manner, restricting its sphere of investigation to the measurable material universe. Those who deny the spiritual world or the existence of God exercise faith that only what can be perceived through the five senses really exists. Science has nothing to say about the spiritual realm, which cannot be measured with scientific instruments. So any scientist who denies a non-material universe has gone beyond the bounds of science—he is making an act of faith. (In fact, many scientists *do* believe that non-material universes exist.)

As scientific reasoning has gained influence in our culture, the Church reminds us that faith is not opposed to science. The two go hand in hand—God speaks to us through his creation (nature, science) and through special revelation (Scripture and Tradition). Far from being blind, faith is a way of seeing reality and of interpreting what we see there. Pope John Paul II's encyclical *Fides et Ratio* ("Faith and Reason") explores the relationship between knowledge gained from science and that from faith. John Paul reminds his readers of St. Augustine's conclusion: I don't try to understand in order to *believe*; I believe so I can *understand*.[3] Faith works that way. So, in fact, does science.

Objection: The hierarchy established the Creed to impose its authority, restrict membership, and control the Church.

True, the hierarchy was involved in the development of the Creed—but *not* to impose or control. The bishops probably developed the original short formulas or "rules of faith," used by catechumens preparing for baptism. As Arianism gained ground, the bishops fought the heresy by developing creedal statements to counteract it. The bishops did the same when protecting the Church from the Modalists, the "Spirit-Fighters," and other such heretical groups.

However, there is a difference between writing a creed to *protect* the faithful and *imposing* a creed on the faithful. When a government passes strict laws controlling prescription drugs, it does so not to impose arbitrary authority but to protect the public from danger. The criminal or unscrupulous doctor might regard the law as government imposition, but the law protects citizens from harm. Besides using the Creed

3. John Paul II, *Fides et Ratio* 16ff.

to prepare catechumens for baptism, bishops formulated it to safeguard the faithful from the ravages of false doctrine.

But what about restricting membership in the Church? The Creed does have the effect of separating those who are in from those who aren't, but every organization or society must have such limitations. The question is: Is that *why* the Creed was written? Of course not. If the Church is truly catholic—open to everyone—then arbitrary restriction of Church membership cannot be the Creed's intent. Rather, the intent of the Creed is to *promote* catholicity by saying, in effect: "This is the faith of the Church, and this is the faith you must agree to. Come join us!"

Objection: The Nicene Creed relies in part on philosophical terms, not Scripture alone, and it therefore rests in part on human opinion.

Tertullian, an ardent Christian, once asked, "What indeed has Athens to do with Jerusalem?"—that is, what does philosophy have to do with faith? Tertullian's answer: nothing! He drew a line between pagan, philosophical premises and divine, biblical revelation.

Tertullian's caution was primarily caused by his desire to protect the Church from the flurry of pagan philosophies that attempted to infiltrate and corrupt Christian doctrine. However, Tertullian himself was very good with words. In fact, his logic and terminology gave the Church much of the philosophical and theological language it still uses to talk about the Trinity. Along with Tertullian, the Church has been very prudent and wise in its use of philosophy to help explain and defend the faith.

As explained earlier, the Creed relies predominantly on Scripture for its teaching about the Trinity. We can easily pick out specific Scripture verses to which the Creed refers. However, there is one major exception—that the Son is *homoousios* (consubstantial) with the Father. The term *homoousios* is a philosophical term that means "the same in being" or "of one substance with." The term was in common use years before the first version of the Nicene Creed, but it became important when Arius and his followers taught that the Son was a creature and so of a different substance from the Father. To refute Arius, the bishops who framed the Creed had to use the language Arius used—to fight fire with fire, so to speak.

Even though at this point the Creed uses a word not found in Scripture, the result *supports* Scripture and explains Jesus' words when he says, "I and the Father are one" (John 10:30).

Appendix One

A SHORT LIST OF CREEDS

This book concentrates on the two commonly accepted versions of the Creed: the Apostles' Creed (used in Rome by the seventh century) and the Nicene Creed (published in A.D. 325 and expanded at Constantinople in A.D. 381).

In response to the heresies that popped up like weeds everywhere in the early Church, bishops and pastors often referred to "the Rule of Faith," a kind of litmus test of fidelity to the gospel. The Rule of Faith outlined belief in the three-fold nature of God and was used to help catechumens prepare for baptism. These statements were short, often limited to naming the Persons of the Trinity. Pope Clement I, Ignatius of Antioch, the *Didache*, and the *Shepherd of Hermas* all used variations of this rule.

By the middle of the second century, bishops felt the need to expand on the simple "Rule of Faith" formulas and began writing longer summaries of the faith for their churches. These became formal creeds, though their use was local or intended for a particular purpose such as combating a particular heresy. Here is a partial list of these creeds, arranged in roughly chronological order:

- Various creeds and hymns embedded in the New Testament (e.g., Phil. 2:5–8; 1 Tim. 3:16)

- Creed of Justin Martyr (A.D. 150), contained in *Apology* I, 13
- Gnostic-infected creed (c. A.D. 150–180)
- Creed of Irenaeus (A.D. 180) in *The Preaching of the Apostles* 6
- Egyptian creed, or the so-called "Der Balizeh" creed (discovered on papyrus in sixth century but dating from the end of the second century)
- North African creed composed by Tertullian (A.D. 213)
- Creed of Hippolytus (A.D. 215–217) in *The Apostolic Tradition* 21, composed as part of a baptismal liturgy
- Creed of Eusebius of Caesarea (A.D. 325), which served as a structural model for the Nicene Creed
- First Creed of Nicaea, with canons condemning Arius (A.D. 325)
- Creed of Arius and Euzosius (A.D. 327), a heretical creed contained in a letter to Emperor Constantine
- Creed of Cyril of Jerusalem (c. A.D. 348)
- Creed of Epiphanius (A.D. 374)
- Creed of the First Council of Constantinople, which expands the Nicene Creed (381)
- Creed of St. Ambrose of Milan (A.D. 397)
- Roman ("Apostles") Creed reported by Rufinus of Aquilaea (A.D. 404)
- Athanasian Creed (attributed to St. Athanasius but composed in Latin in the West long after Athanasius died)
- "Faith of Damasus," or creed attributed to Pope

Damasus I (who died in A.D. 384; it actually originates in southern Gaul in the fifth century)

- Creed of the Eleventh Council of Toledo (A.D. 675)
- Creed of the Fourth Lateran Council (A.D. 1215) in response to the Albigensian and Catharist heresies
- Creed of the Second Council of Lyons, also called the "Profession of Faith of Michael Paleologus" (1274)
- Profession of Faith of Pius IV (1564) during the Council of Trent as part of a profession of faith of all Catholic bishops
- Creed of Pope Paul VI (1968) in opposition to dissent entering the Church following the Second Vatican Council

Appendix Two

GLOSSARY

Analogy: Figurative language that emphasizes what two things have in common. Analogy provides a way to learn about what we don't know by drawing comparisons with what we do know. The Bible often uses analogical language when speaking of God.

Apprehension: In theology, perception—or the simple recognition that a fact exists. God is knowable on this level.

Arianism: A fourth-century heresy that held that the Son of God is a creature, not eternal and not of the same nature as the Father. The name of the heresy came from its proponent, Arius (256–336).

Article: In the structure of the Creed a clause, phrase, or sentence dealing with a major topic; for example, the article that summarizes belief about the Father.

Atheism: Rejection of belief in the existence of a divinity. Systematic atheists have philosophical reasons for their disbelief. Practical atheists may claim a belief in God but act as if God does not exist. Agnosticism is the belief that one cannot know whether God exists or not, a form of systematic atheism.

Blasphemy: As defined by the Catechism, the act of "uttering against God—inwardly or outwardly—words of hatred, reproach, or defiance, in speaking ill of God, in failing in respect toward him in one's speech, [or] in misusing God's name."[1]

Catechumen: An unbaptized person undergoing instruction in preparation for baptism.

Charism: A "special grace" of the Holy Spirit intended for the building up of the Church; for example, utterance of prophecy, working of miracles, or prayer in tongues. According to the Catechism, charisms are to be received with gratitude, discerned carefully, exercised in a spirit of charity, and submitted to the authority of the Church.[2]

Comprehension: In theology, complete understanding of a mystery. Human beings cannot fully comprehend or grasp God, because God who is infinite is beyond our understanding. We can have true, but not exhaustive, knowledge.

Consubstantial: Having the same substance as, or one in being with. A technical term applied to the Persons of the

---

1. CCC 2148.
2. Ibid., 798–801.

Trinity, who share sameness of being while being distinct in Person.

Demiurge: In Platonic thought, a half-god created by the divine "Father beyond All Knowing" whose role is to give shape to formless matter. Arians essentially placed the Son in the role of the Demiurge.

Docetism: The heresy that holds that the humanity of the Son is an illusion. Docetists believed it was impossible for God, a pure spirit, to join with matter.

Economy: In theology, the way in which the Trinity reveals itself in human history and manages the various aspects in the process of salvation.

Gnosticism: A religious system that combined elements of Christianity and paganism with the idea that one who knew the secret knowledge, the pattern of ascent toward God, could attain salvation by following it. Within this system, matter was evil and spirit was good.

Gospel: A proclamation of "good news" (from Old English "god spell," hence gospel) of salvation from sin, told in the form of a story of Jesus' life and ministry. The term Gospels refer to the four New Testament accounts of the life of Christ: Matthew, Mark, Luke, and John. The first three are called "synoptic Gospels" because their accounts are seen "with the same eye"—that is, from the same general point of view—and bear extensive similarities of content and arrangement (with some notable dissimilarities as well).

Grace: Unmerited divine favor, the free and undeserved help, called "actual grace," that God gives us to respond to his call to become his children, adoptive sons, partakers of the divine nature and eternal life. Participation in the very life of God is called "sanctifying grace."[3]

Marcionism: An early heresy that rejected the Old Testament and a good portion of the New Testament. Claiming to follow Paul, it taught that Christianity was a religion of love without law. Its followers baptized only unmarried people.

Messiah: Anointed—"Christ" in Greek. A human being (such as a king) anointed by a prophet or someone speaking on God's behalf to save God's people from a danger. Specifically, it is the Hebrew title for the promised deliverer of the Jewish people and ultimately all of mankind, fulfilled in Jesus Christ.[4]

Modalism: A heresy that tried to uphold the oneness of God by denying the reality of the Holy Trinity. It taught that God has three different "modes" or ways of manifesting

---

3. Ibid., 1996–1999.
4. Ibid., 436–440.

himself—sometimes as Father, sometimes as Son, and sometimes as Holy Spirit.[5]

Monotheism: Having to do with belief in one God. Jews, Christians, and Muslims are monotheists.

Mystery: In theology, a reality that has been revealed but is not entirely understandable to the human mind, such as the nature of Christ or of the Church. The term is sometimes used to refer to the sacraments, which are signs that point to and activate mysteries.

Orthodoxy: Literally, "right belief," the habit of faith according to the teaching of the Church founded on the apostles.

Orthopraxis: Literally, "right conduct," the habitual practice of Christian morality.

Paraclete: Greek for "one who comes alongside"; namely, an advocate, counselor, or defense attorney. Paraclete is a title usually applied to the Holy Spirit, although Jesus is also described as a paraclete or counselor.

Particular church: Usually, a jurisdiction of an area's churches such as a diocese or eparchy; a "community of the Christian faithful in communion of faith and sacraments with their bishop ordained in apostolic succession."[6]

---

5. Ibid., 254.
6. Ibid., 833.

Patripassianism: The heretical belief that the Father suffered on the cross in the human form of Jesus.

Polytheism: The belief that there is more than one god; for example, ancient Egyptians, Greeks, and Romans were polytheists.

Premillenialism: The belief in the personal coming of Christ in glory to inaugurate a millennial reign of Christ on earth before the Final Judgment. The objection of Augustine and other Fathers caused its rejection until its reappearance in some circles in the seventeenth century.

Proceed: To "originate" or "come out from." The verb refers to the manner in which one Person of the Holy Trinity has his source from or within another. The Son proceeds from the Father; the Spirit proceeds from both the Father and the Son. In its noun form, the term is procession, or "a coming forth."

Rapture: The belief that Christ will secretly return before the Last Day to snatch up the elect, both the dead and living, to heaven. This is a common belief among Protestants known as Dispensationalists. It originated in the nineteenth century and is rejected by the Catholic Church.

Resurrection: The raising of a person to a new dimension of both physical and spiritual life. This revivification is permanent, not temporary.

Revelation: Literally, the "pulling back" of a veil. The process by which God unfolds to human beings certain characteristics of his own nature and what his plan is for the human race.

Rite: Strictly, a liturgical function. In the broadest sense, a grouping of historical churches in communion with the pope with a distinctive hierarchical, liturgical, and theological tradition. The word comes from the Latin ritus, meaning "practice."

"Rule of faith": In ancient times, a standard for interpreting Scripture, which later evolved into the creeds we have now. This "rule" operated as a way of identifying the true faith and established the boundaries of personal conduct.

Spirate: To "breathe out" from another source. Like the verb proceed, this word refers to the "origin" of the Holy Spirit from within the Godhead. The noun form of the word is spiration, or a "breathing out" or procession of the Spirit.

Symbol of faith: Another name for the Creed, so called because it functions as a sign of recognition and communion between believers professing the same faith. A summary of the principal truths of the faith.

Trinity: A term coined to signify a three-ness in unity; one God existing as three Persons in a single divine nature. Belief in a Trinity in this sense is uniquely Christian.

Appendix Three

CITATIONS

Job

1:6
33:4

Psalms

2:7
8:4
10:16
14:7
18:6–13
19:1
19:12–13
22:6
24:10
33:6
40:7–8
51:1–3
69:5
80:2
82:1
95:3
102:18–19
104:30
110:1
115:4–6
119:141
135:15–18
138 (all)
139 (all)
144:5

Proverbs

8:22–31

Wisdom

2:13–18
7:22–25
13:1ff 18:13

Sirach

23:1
24:3–9

Isaiah

5:16
6:3
6:5–7
7:14
11:1–3
13:6
29:19
42:1–4
42:8
43:6
44:6
45:12–21
57:16
63:10

Jeremiah

11:4
23:30–32
31:9
31:35

Ezekiel

1:4–20
28:22
37:1–14
47:1–10

Ephesians

1:2
1:9–12
1:22–23
2:11–16
2:19–22
3:8–10
3:15
4:4–6
4:8–10
4:11–13
4:30
5:23, 25–27

Philippians

1:19
1:27–2:3
2:5–11
3:10–11
3:20–21

Colossians

1:5–6
1:12
1:15–19
2:9

1 Thessalonians

1:1
1:10
3:13
4:13
4:14
4:16–17
5:20–21

2 Thessalonians

2:13

1 Timothy

1:3–7
3 (all)
3:15
3:16
4:14

2 Timothy

2:2
3:16–17
4:1–5

Titus

1:5ff

Hebrews

1:1–3
1:5
1:8–12
4:14
7:28
9:15
9:27–28
10:7
10:15
12:10
12:14

1 Peter

1:15–16
1:18–19
2:5
3:6
3:18–22
4:17

2 Peter

1:4
1:17
1:20–21
3:13
3:15–16

1 John

1:1–4
1:7
2:2
2:23
3:2
4:2
4:9
4:13
4:14
4:18
5:4
5:6–8
5:9–10
5:20

Revelation

1:8
2:16

Catechism of the Catholic Church